John Adams

Acts passed at the first session of the Congress of the United States

of America

Begun and held at the city of New-York

John Adams

Acts passed at the first session of the Congress of the United States of America
Begun and held at the city of New-York

ISBN/EAN: 9783337175832

Printed in Europe, USA, Canada, Australia, Japan

Cover: Foto ©Suzi / pixelio.de

More available books at **www.hansebooks.com**

ACTS

PASSED AT THE

FIRST SESSION

OF THE

CONGRESS

OF THE

UNITED STATES

OF

AMERICA,

BEGUN AND HELD AT THE CITY OF NEW-YORK,
ON WEDNESDAY THE FOURTH OF MARCH,
IN THE YEAR M,DCC,LXXXIX:

AND OF THE
INDEPENDENCE OF THE UNITED STATES
THE THIRTEENTH.

PHILADELPHIA:
PRINTED BY FRANCIS CHILDS AND JOHN SWAINE,
PRINTERS TO THE UNITED STATES.
M,DCC;XCI.

CONSTITUTION

OF THE

UNITED STATES.

WE, The People of the United States, in order to form a more perfect Union, establish Justice, insure domestic Tranquility, provide for the common Defence, promote the general Welfare, and secure the Blessings of Liberty to ourselves and our Posterity, DO ORDAIN AND ESTABLISH this CONSTITUTION for the UNITED STATES of AMERICA.

ARTICLE I.

Sect. 1. ALL legislative powers herein granted, shall be vested in a Congress of the United States, which shall consist of a Senate and House of Representatives.

Sect. 2. The House of Representatives shall be composed of members chosen every second year by the people of the several states; and the electors in each state shall have the qualifications requisite for electors of the most numerous branch of the state legislature.

No person shall be a Representative who shall not have attained to the age of twenty-five years, and been seven years a citizen of the United States, and who shall not, when elected, be an inhabitant of that state in which he shall be chosen.

Representatives and direct taxes shall be apportioned among the several states which may be included within this Union, according to their respective numbers, which shall be determined by adding to the whole number of free perſons, including thoſe bound to ſervice for a term of years, and excluding Indians not taxed, three fifths of all other perſons. The actual enumeration ſhall be made within three years after the firſt meeting of the Congreſs of the United States, and within every ſubſequent term of ten years, in ſuch manner as they ſhall by law direct. The number of Repreſentatives ſhall not exceed one for every thirty thouſand, but each ſtate ſhall have at leaſt one Repreſentative; and until ſuch enumeration ſhall be made, the ſtate of New-Hampſhire ſhall be entitled to chuſe three; Maſſachuſetts, eight; Rhode-Iſland and Providence Plantations, one; Connecticut, five; New-York, ſix; New-Jerſey, four; Pennſylvania, eight; Delaware, one; Maryland, ſix; Virginia, ten; North-Carolina, five; South-Carolina, five; and Georgia, three.

When vacancies happen in the repreſentation from any ſtate, the executive authority thereof ſhall iſſue writs of election to fill ſuch vacancies.

The Houſe of Repreſentatives ſhall chuſe their Speaker and other officers; and ſhall have the ſole power of impeachment.

Sect. 3. The Senate of the United States ſhall be compoſed of two Senators from each ſtate, choſen by the legiſlature thereof, for ſix years; and each Senator ſhall have one vote.

Immediately after they ſhall be aſſembled in conſequence of the firſt election, they ſhall be divided as equally as may be into three claſſes. The ſeats of the Senators of the firſt claſs ſhall be vacated at the expiration of the ſecond year, of the ſecond claſs at the expiration of the fourth year, and of the third claſs at the expiration of the ſixth year, ſo that one third may be choſen every ſecond year; and if vacancies happen by reſignation, or otherwiſe, during the receſs of the legiſlature of any ſtate, the executive thereof may make temporary appointments until the next meeting of the legiſlature, which ſhall then fill ſuch vacancies.

No perſon ſhall be a Senator who ſhall not have attained to the age of thirty years, and been nine years a citizen of the United States, and who shall not when elected, be an inhabitant of that state for which he shall be chosen.

The Vice-President of the United States shall be President of the Senate, but shall have no vote, unless they be equally divided.

The Senate shall chuse their other officers, and also a President *pro tempore*, in the absence of the Vice-President, or when he shall exercise the office of President of the United States.

The Senate shall have the sole power to try all impeachments. When sitting for that purpose, they shall be on oath or affirmation. When the President of the United States is tried, the Chief Justice shall preside: and no person shall be convicted without the concurrence of two thirds of the members present.

Judgment in cases of impeachment shall not extend further than to removal from office, and disqualification to hold and enjoy any office of honor, trust or profit under the United States; but the party convicted shall nevertheless be liable and subject to indictment, trial, judgment and punishment according to law.

Sect. 4. The times, places and manner of holding elections for Senators and Representatives, shall be prescribed in each state by the legislature thereof: But the Congress may at any time by law make or alter such regulations, except as to the places of chusing Senators.

The Congress shall assemble at least once in every year, and such meeting shall be on the first Monday in December, unless they shall by law appoint a different day.

Sect. 5. Each House shall be the judge of the elections, returns and qualifications of its own members, and a majority of each shall constitute a quorum to do business; but a smaller number may adjourn from day to day, and may be authorized to compel the attendance of absent members, in such manner, and under such penalties as each House may provide.

Each House may determine the rules of its proceedings, punish its members for disorderly behaviour, and, with the concurrence of two thirds, expel a member.

Each House shall keep a journal of its proceedings, and from time to time publish the same, excepting such parts as may in their judgment require secrecy; and the yeas and nays of the members of either House on any question, shall, at the desire of one fifth of those present, be entered on the journal.

Neither House, during the session of Congress, shall without the consent of the other, adjourn for more than three days, nor to any other place than that in which the two Houses shall be sitting.

Sect. 6. The Senators and Representatives shall receive a compensation for their services, to be ascertained by law, and paid out of the treasury of the United States. They shall in all cases, except treason, felony and breach of the peace, be privileged from arrest during their attendance at the session of their respective Houses, and in going to and returning from the same; and for any speech or debate in either House, they shall not be questioned in any other place.

No Senator or Representative shall, during the time for which he was elected, be appointed to any civil office under the authority of the United States, which shall have been created, or the emoluments whereof shall have been encreased during such time; and no person holding any office under the United States, shall be a member of either House during his continuance in office.

Sect. 7. All bills for raising revenue shall orginate in the House of Representatives; but the Senate may propose or concur with amendments as on other bills.

Every bill which shall have passed the House of Representatives and the Senate, shall, before it become a law, be presented to the President of the United States: If he approve he shall sign it; but if not he shall return it, with his objections, to that House in which it shall have originated, who shall enter the objections at large on their journal, and proceed to reconsider it. If after such reconsideration, two thirds of that House shall agree to pass the bill, it shall be sent, together with the objections, to the other House, by which it shall likewise be reconsidered, and if approved by two thirds of that House, it shall become a law. But in all such cases, the votes of both Houses shall be determined by yeas and nays ; and the names of the persons voting for and against the bill, shall be entered on the journal of each House respectively. If any bill shall not be returned by the President within ten days (Sundays excepted) after it shall have been presented to him, the same shall be a law, in like manner as if he had signed it, unless the Congress by their adjournment prevent its return, in which case it shall not be a law.

Every order, resolution or vote to which the concurrence of the Senate and House of Representatives may be necessary (except on a question of adjournment) shall be presented to the President of the United States ; and before the same shall take effect, shall be approved by him, or being disapproved by him, shall be repassed by two thirds of the Senate and House of Representatives, according to the rules and limitations prescribed in the case of a bill.

Sect. 8. The Congress shall have power—

To lay and collect taxes, duties, imposts and excises, to pay the debts and provide for the common defence and general welfare of the United States ; but all duties, imposts and excises, shall be uniform throughout the United States:

To borrow money on the credit of the United States :

To regulate commerce with foreign nations, and among the several states, and with the Indian tribes :

To establish an uniform rule of naturalization, and uniform laws on the subject of bankruptcies throughout the United States :

To coin money, regulate the value thereof, and of foreign coin, and fix the standard of weights and measures :

To provide for the punishment of counterfeiting the securities and current coin of the United States :

To establish post-offices and post-roads :

To promote the progress of science and useful arts by securing for limited times to authors and inventors the exclusive right to their respective writings and discoveries :

To constitute tribunals inferior to the supreme court :

To define and punish piracies and felonies committed on the high seas, and offences against the law of nations:

To declare war, grant letters of marque and reprisal, and make rules concerning captures on land and water:

To raise and support armies; but no appropriation of money to that use shall be for a longer term than two years:

To provide and maintain a navy:

To make rules for the government and regulation of the land and naval forces:

To provide for calling forth the militia to execute the laws of the Union, suppress insurrections and repel invasions:

To provide for organizing, arming, and disciplining the militia, and for governing such part of them as may be employed in the service of the United States, reserving to the states respectively, the appointment of the officers, and the authority of training the militia according to the discipline prescribed by Congress:

To exercise exclusive legislation in all cases whatsoever, over such district (not exceeding ten miles square) as may by cession of particular states, and the acceptance of Congress, become the seat of the government of the United States, and to exercise like authority over all places purchased by the consent of the legislature of the state in which the same shall be, for the erection of forts, magazines, arsenals, dock-yards, and other needful buildings:—And

To make all laws which shall be necessary and proper for carrying into execution the foregoing powers, and all other powers vested by this Constitution in the government of the United States, or in any department or officer thereof.

Sect. 9. The migration or importation of such persons as any of the States now existing shall think proper to admit, shall not be prohibited by the Congress prior to the year one thousand eight hundred and eight; but a tax or duty may be imposed on such importation, not exceeding ten dollars for each person.

The privilege of the writ of *habeas corpus* shall not be suspended, unless when in cases of rebellion or invasion the public safety may require it.

No bill of attainder or *ex post facto* law shall be passed.

No capitation, or other direct tax shall be laid, unless in proportion to the *census* or enumeration herein before directed to be taken.

No tax or duty shall be laid on articles exported from any state. No preference shall be given by any regulation of commerce or revenue to the ports of one state over those of another: nor shall vessels bound to, or from, one state be obliged to enter, clear, or pay duties in another.

No money shall be drawn from the treasury, but in consequence of appropriations made by law; and a regular statement and account of the receipts and expenditures of all public money shall be published from time to time.

No title of nobility shall be granted by the United States: and no person holding any office of profit or trust under them, shall, without the consent of the Congress, accept of any present, emolument, office, or title of any kind whatever, from any king, prince or foreign state.

Sect. 10. No state shall enter into any treaty, alliance or confederation; grant letters of marque and reprisal; coin money; emit bills of credit; make any thing but gold and silver coin a tender in payment of debts; pass any bill of attainder, *ex post facto* law, or law impairing the obligation of contracts, or grant any title of nobility.

No state shall, without the consent of the Congress, lay any imposts or duties on imports or exports, except what may be absolutely necessary for executing its inspection laws; and the net produce of all duties and imposts, laid by any state on imports or exports, shall be for the use of the treasury of the United States; and all such laws shall be subject to the revision and controul of the Congress. No state shall, without the consent of Congress, lay any duty of tonnage, keep troops, or ships of war in time of peace, enter into any agreement or compact with another state, or with a foreign power, or engage in war, unless actually invaded, or in such imminent danger as will not admit of delay.

ARTICLE II.

Sect. 1. The executive power shall be vested in a President of the United States of America. He shall hold his office during the term of four years, and together with the Vice-President, chosen for the same term, be elected as follows:

Each state shall appoint, in such manner as the legislature thereof may direct, a number of electors, equal to the whole number of Senators and Representatives to which the state may be entitled in the Congress: but no Senator or Representative, or person holding an office of trust or profit under the United States, shall be appointed an elector.

The electors shall meet in their respective states, and vote by ballot for two persons, of whom one at least shall not be an inhabitant of the same state with themselves. And they shall make a list of all the persons voted for, and of the number of votes for each; which list they shall sign and certify, and transmit, sealed, to the seat of the government of the United States, directed to the President of the Senate. The President of the Senate shall, in the presence of the Senate and House of Representatives, open all the certificates, and the votes shall then be counted. The person having the greatest number of votes shall be the President, if such number be a majority of the whole number of electors appointed; and if there be more than one who have such majority, and have an equal number of votes, then the House of Representatives shall immediately chuse by ballot one of them for President; and if no person have a majority, then from the five highest on the list the said House shall in like manner chuse the President. But in chusing the President, the votes shall be taken by states, the representation from each state having one vote; a quorum for this purpose shall consist of a member or members from two thirds of the states, and a majority of all the states shall be necessary to a choice. In every case, after the choice of the President, the person having the greatest number of votes of the electors shall be the Vice-President. But if there should remain two or more who have equal votes, the

Senate shall chuse from them by ballot the Vice-President.

The Congress may determine the time of chusing the electors, and the day on which they shall give their votes, which day shall be the same throughout the United States.

No person except a natural born citizen, or a citizen of the United States, at the time of the adoption of this Constitution, shall be eligible to the office of President; neither shall any person be eligible to that office who shall not have attained to the age of thirty-five years, and been fourteen years a resident within the United States.

In case of the removal of the President from office, or of his death, resignation, or inability to discharge the powers and duties of the said office, the same shall devolve on the Vice-President; and the Congress may by law provide for the case of removal, death, resignation or inability, both of the President and Vice-President, declaring what officer shall then act as President; and such officer shall act accordingly, until the disability be removed, or a President shall be elected.

The President shall, at stated times, receive for his services, a compensation, which shall neither be increased nor diminished during the period for which he shall have been elected; and he shall not receive within that period any other emolument from the United States, or any of them.

Before he enter on the execution of his office, he shall take the following oath or affirmation:

" I do solemnly swear (or affirm) that I will faithfully execute the office of President of the United States; and will, to the best of my ability, preserve, protect and defend the Constitution of the United States."

Sect. 2. The President shall be commander in chief of the army and navy of the United States, and of the militia of the several states, when called into the actual service of the United States; he may require the opinion, in writing, of the principal officer in each of the executive departments, upon any subject relating to the duties of their respective offices, and he shall have power to grant reprieves and pardons for offences against the United States, except in cases of impeachment.

C

He shall have power, by and with the advice and consent of the Senate, to make treaties, provided two thirds of the Senators present concur; and he shall nominate, and by and with the advice and consent of the Senate, shall appoint ambassadors, other public ministers and consuls; judges of the supreme court, and all other officers of the United States, whose appointments are not herein otherwise provided for, and which shall be established by law. But the Congress may by law vest the appointment of such inferior officers, as they think proper, in the President alone, in the courts of law, or in the heads of departments.

The President shall have power to fill up all vacancies that may happen during the recess of the Senate, by granting commissions which shall expire at the end of their next session.

Sect. 3. He shall from time to time give to the Congress information of the state of the Union, and recommend to their consideration such measures as he shall judge necessary and expedient: He may on extraordinary occasions, convene both Houses, or either of them; and in case of disagreement between them, with respect to the time of adjournment, he may adjourn them to such time as he shall think proper: He shall receive ambassadors and other public ministers: He shall take care that the laws be faithfully executed, and shall commission all the officers of the United States.

Sect. 4. The President, Vice-President, and all civil officers of the United States, shall be removed from office on impeachment for, and conviction of, treason, bribery, or other high crimes and misdemeanors.

ARTICLE III.

Sect. 1. The judicial power of the United States, shall be vested in one supreme court, and in such inferior courts as the Congress may from time to time ordain and establish. The judges, both of the supreme and inferior court, shall hold their offices during good behaviour; and shall, at stated times, receive for their services, a compensation, which shall not be diminished during their continuance in office.

Sect. 2. The judicial power shall extend to all cases, in law and equity, arising under this Constitution, the laws of the United States, and treaties made, or which shall be made, under their authority; to all cases affecting ambassadors, other public ministers, and consuls; to all cases of admiralty and maritime jurisdiction; to controversies to which the United States shall be a party; to controversies between two or more states; between a state and citizens of another state; between citizens of different states; between citizens of the same state claiming lands under grants of different states; and between a state, or the citizens thereof, and foreign states, citizens or subjects.

In all cases affecting ambassadors, other public ministers and consuls, and those in which a state shall be a party, the supreme court shall have original jurisdiction. In all the other cases before mentioned, the supreme court shall have appellate jurisdiction, both as to law and fact, with such exceptions, and under such regulations as the Congress shall make.

The trial of all crimes, except in cases of impeachment, shall be by jury; and such trial shall be held in the state where the said crimes shall have been committed; but when not committed within any state, the trial shall be at such place or places as the Congress may by law have directed.

Sect. 3. Treason against the United States, shall consist only in levying war against them, or in adhering to their enemies, giving them aid and comfort. No person shall be convicted of treason unless on the testimony of two witnesses to the same overt act, or on confession in open court.

The Congress shall have power to declare the punishment of treason; but no attainder of treason shall work corruption of blood, or forfeiture, except during the life of the person attainted.

ARTICLE IV.

Sect. 1. Full faith and credit shall be given in each state to the public acts, records and judicial proceedings of every other state. And the Congress may by general laws prescribe the manner in which such acts, records and proceedings shall be proved, and the effect thereof.

Sect. 2. The citizens of each state shall be entitled to all privileges and immunities of citizens in the several states.

A person charged in any state with treason, felony, or other crime, who shall flee from justice, and be found in another state, shall, on demand of the executive authority of the state from which he fled, be delivered up, to be removed to the state having jurisdiction of the crime.

No person held to service or labour in one state, under the laws thereof, escaping into another, shall, in consequence of any law or regulation therein, be discharged from such service or labour, but shall be delivered up on claim of the party to whom such service or labour may be due.

Sect. 3. New states may be admitted by the Congress into this Union; but no new state shall be formed or erected within the jurisdiction of any other state; nor any state be formed by the junction of two or more states, or parts of states, without the consent of the legislatures of the states concerned as well as of the Congress.

The Congress shall have power to dispose of and make all needful rules and regulations respecting the territory or other property belonging to the United States; and nothing in this Constitution shall be so construed as to prejudice any claims of the United States, or of any particular state.

Sect. 4. The United States shall guarantee to every state in this Union a republican form of government, and shall protect each of them against invasion; and on application of the legislature, or of the executive (when the legislature cannot be convened) against domestic violence.

ARTICLE V.

The Congress, whenever two thirds of both Houses shall deem it necessary, shall propose amendments to this Constitution, or, on the application of the legislatures of two thirds of the several states, shall call a convention for proposing amendments, which, in either case, shall be valid to all intents and purposes, as part of this Constitution, when ratified by the legislatures of three fourths of the several states, or by conventions in three fourths thereof, as the one or the other mode of ratification may be proposed by the Congress: Provided, that no amendment which may be made prior to the year one thousand eight hundred and eight, shall in any manner affect the first and fourth clauses in the ninth section of the first article; and that no state, without its consent, shall be deprived of its equal suffrage in the Senate.

ARTICLE VI.

All debts contracted and engagements entered into, before the adoption of this Constitution, shall be as valid against the United States under this Constitution, as under the confederation.

This Constitution, and the laws of the United States which shall be made in pursuance thereof; and all treaties made, or which shall be made, under the authority of the United States, shall be the supreme law of the land; and the judges in every state shall be bound thereby, any thing in the Constitution or laws of any state to the contrary notwithstanding.

The Senators and Representatives before mentioned, and the members of the several state legislatures, and all executive and judicial officers, both of the United States and of the several states, shall be bound by oath or affirmation, to support this Constitution; but no religious test shall ever be required as a qualification to any office or public trust under the United States.

ARTICLE VII.

The ratification of the conventions of nine states, shall be sufficient for the establishment of this Constitution between the states so ratifying the same.

DONE in Convention, by the unanimous consent of the States present, the seventeenth day of September, in the year of our Lord one thousand seven hundred and eighty-seven, and of the independence of the United States of America the twelfth. In witness whereof we have hereunto subscribed our Names.

GEORGE WASHINGTON, PRESIDENT,
And Deputy from VIRGINIA.

New-Hampshire, { John Langdon,
Nicholas Gilman.

Massachusetts,	Nathaniel Gorham, Rufus King.
Connecticut,	William Samuel Johnson, Roger Sherman.
New-York,	Alexander Hamilton.
New-Jersey,	William Livingston, David Brearly, William Patterson, Jonathan Dayton.
Pennsylvania,	Benjamin Franklin, Thomas Mifflin, Robert Morris, George Clymer, Thomas Fitzsimons, Jared Ingersol, James Wilson, Gouverneur Morris.
Delaware,	George Read, Gunning Bedford, junior, John Dickinson, Richard Bassett, Jacob Broom.
Maryland,	James M'Henry, Daniel of St. Thomas Jenifer, Daniel Carroll.
Virginia,	John Blair, James Madison, junior.
North-Carolina,	William Blount, Richard Dobbs Spaight, Hugh Williamson.
South-Carolina,	John Rutledge, Charles Cotesworth Pinckney, Charles Pinckney, Pierce Butler.
Georgia,	William Few, Abraham Baldwin.
Attest.	WILLIAM JACKSON, *Secretary.*

In CONVENTION,

Monday, *September* 17, 1787.

PRESENT,

The States of NEW-HAMPSHIRE, MASSACHUSETTS, CONNECTICUT, Mr. *Hamilton*, from NEW-YORK, NEW-JERSEY, PENNSYLVANIA, DELAWARE, MARYLAND, VIRGINIA, NORTH-CAROLINA, SOUTH-CAROLINA, and GEORGIA:

RESOLVED,

THAT the preceding Conftitution be laid before the United States in Congrefs affembled, and that it is the opinion of this Convention, that it fhould afterwards be fubmitted to a Convention of Delegates, chofen in each State by the people thereof, under the recommendation of its Legiflature, for their affent and ratification; and that each Convention affenting to, and ratifying the fame, fhould give notice thereof to the United States in Congrefs affembled.

Refolved, That it is the opinion of this Convention, that as foon as the Conventions of nine States fhall have ratified this Conftitution, the United States in Congrefs affembled fhould fix a day on which electors fhould be appointed by the States which fhall have ratified the fame, and a day on which the electors fhould affemble to vote for the Prefident, and the time and place for commencing proceedings under this Conftitution. That after fuch publication the electors fhould be appointed, and the Senators and Reprefentatives elected. That the electors fhould meet on the day fixed for the election of the Prefident, and fhould tranfmit their votes certified, figned, fealed and directed, as the Conftitution requires, to the Secretary of the United States in Congrefs affembled. That the Senators and Reprefentatives fhould convene at the time and place affigned. That the Senators fhould appoint a Prefident of the Senate, for the fole purpofe of receiving, opening and counting the votes for Prefident; and, that after he fhall be chosen, the Congress, together with the President, should, without delay, proceed to execute this Constitution.

By the Unanimous Order of the Convention,
  GEORGE WASHINGTON, *President.*
WILLIAM JACKSON, *Secretary.*

IN CONVENTION,
SEPTEMBER, 17, 1787.

SIR,

WE have now the honor to submit to the consideration of the United States in Congress assembled, that Constitution which has appeared to us the most advisable.

The friends of our country have long seen and desired, that the power of making war, peace and treaties; that of levying money and regulating commerce, and the correspondent executive and judicial authorities, should be fully and effectually vested in the general government of the Union: But the impropriety of delegating such extensive trust to one body of men is evident—Hence results the necessity of a different organization.

It is obviously impracticable in the federal government of these States, to secure all rights of independent sovereignty to each, and yet provide for the interest and safety of all—Individuals entering into society, must give up a share of liberty to preserve the rest. The magnitude of the sacrifice must depend as well on situation and circumstance, as on the object to be obtained. It is at all times difficult to draw with precision the line between those rights which must be surrendered, and those which may be reserved; and on the present occasion this difficulty was encreased by a difference among the several States as to their situation, extent, habits, and particular interests.

In all our deliberations on this subject we kept steadily in our view, that which appears to us the greatest interest of every true American, the confolidation of our Union, in which is involved our profperity, felicity, fafety, perhaps our national exiftence. This important confideration ferioufly and deeply imprefled on our minds, led each State in the Convention to be lefs rigid on points of inferior magnitude, than might have been otherwife expected; and thus the Conftitution, which we now prefent, is the refult of a fpirit of amity, and of that mutual deference and conceffion which the peculiarity of our political fituation rendered indifpenfible.

That it will meet the full and entire approbation of every State is not perhaps to be expected; but each will doubtlefs confider, that had her intereft been alone confulted, the confequences might have been particularly difagreeable or injurious to others; that it is liable to as few exceptions as could reafonably have been expected we hope and believe; that it may promote the lafting welfare of that country fo dear to us all, and fecure her freedom and happinefs, is our moft ardent wifh.

With great refpect,

We have the Honor to be,

SIR,

Your Excellency's moft

Obedient and humble Servants,

GEORGE WASHINGTON, *Prefident.*

By unanimous Order of the Convention.

His Excellency
 The PRESIDENT of Congrefs.

ACTS

OF

CONGRESS.

CHAPTER I.

An ACT *to regulate the Time and Manner of administering certain* OATHS.

Section 1. BE it enacted by the SENATE and REPRESENTATIVES *of the United States of America in Congress assembled*, That the oath or affirmation required by the sixth article of the Constitution of the United States, shall be administered in the form following, to wit, "I, A. B. do solemnly swear or affirm (as the case may be) that I will support the Constitution of the United States." The said oath or affirmation shall be administered within three days after the passing of this act, by any one member of the Senate, to the President of the Senate, and by him to all the members, and to the Secretary ; and by the Speaker of the House of Representatives, to all the members who have not taken a similar oath, by virtue of a particular resolution of the said House, and to the Clerk : And in case of the absence of any member from the service of either House, at the time prescribed for taking the said oath or affirmation, the same shall be administered to such member, when he shall appear to take his seat.

Sec. 2. *And be it further enacted*, That at the first session of Congress after every general election of

<small>Oath to support the constitution the form of.

To be administered to the president, members and secretary of senate, and to members and clerk of the house of representatives.</small>

To members of senate and house of representatives hereafter elected and when.

Representatives, the oath or affirmation aforesaid, shall be administered by any one member of the House of Representatives to the Speaker; and by him to all the members present, and to the Clerk, previous to entering on any other business; and to the members who shall afterwards appear, previous to taking their seats. The President of the Senate for the time being, shall also administer the said oath or affirmation to each Senator who shall hereafter be elected, previous to his taking his seat: And in any future case of a President of the Senate, who shall not have taken the said oath or affirmation, the same shall be administered to him by any one of the members of the Senate.

To members of state legislatures, and to all executive & judicial officers of the several states,

Sec. 3. *And be it further enacted,* That the members of the several state legislatures, at the next sessions of the said legislatures respectively, and all executive and judicial officers of the several states, who have been heretofore chosen or appointed, or who shall be chosen or appointed before the first day of August next, and who shall then be in office, shall, within one month thereafter, take the same oath or affirmation, except where they shall have taken it before; which may be administered by any person authorised by the law of the state, in which such office shall be holden, to administer oaths.

and when.

And the members of the several state legislatures, and all executive and judicial officers of the several states, who shall be chosen or appointed after the said first day of August, shall, before they proceed to execute the duties of their respective offices, take the foregoing oath or affirmation, which shall be administered by the person or persons, who by the law of the state shall be authorised to administer the oath of office; and the person or persons so administering the oath hereby required to be taken, shall cause a record or certificate thereof to be made, in the same manner, as by the law of the state, he or they, shall be directed to record or certify the oath of office.

Sec. 4. *And be it further enacted,* That all officers appointed, or hereafter to be appointed under the authority of the United States, shall, before they act in their respective offices, take the same oath or affirmation, which shall be administered by the person or persons who shall be authorised by law to administer to such officers their respective oaths of office; and such officers shall incur the same penalties in case of failure, as shall be imposed by law in case of failure in taking their respective oaths of office.

To all officers of the U. States, or to be appointed before they act

Sec. 5. *And be it further enacted,* That the Secretary of the Senate, and the Clerk of the House of Representatives for the time being, shall, at the time of taking the oath or affirmation aforesaid, each take an oath or affirmation in the words following, to wit; "I, A. B. Secretary of the Senate, or Clerk of the House of Representatives (as the case may be) of the United States of America, do solemnly swear or affirm, that I will truly and faithfully discharge the duties of my said office, to the best of my knowledge and abilities.

Oath of office, secretary of senate and clerk of the house of representatives.

FREDERICK AUGUSTUS MUHLENBERG,
Speaker of the House of Representatives.

JOHN ADAMS, *Vice-President of the United States, and President of the Senate.*

APPROVED, June 1, 1789.
GEORGE WASHINGTON,
President of the United States.

CHAPTER II.

An ACT *for laying a* DUTY *on* GOODS, WARES, *and* MERCHANDIZES *imported into the United States.*

Section 1. WHEREAS it is necessary for the support of government, for the discharge of the debts of the United States, and

Recital.

the encouragement and protection of manufactures, that duties be laid on goods, wares and merchandizes imported:

Be it enacted by the Senate *and* House *of* Representatives *of the United States of America in Congress assembled,* That from and after the first day of August next ensuing, the several duties herein after mentioned shall be laid on the following goods, wares and merchandizes imported into the United States from any foreign port or place, that is to say:

Specific duties on certain enumerated articles.

On all distilled spirits of Jamaica proof, imported from any kingdom or country whatsoever, per gallon, ten cents.
On all other distilled spirits, per gallon, eight cents.
On molasses, per gallon, two and a half cents.
On Madeira wine, per gallon, eighteen cents.
On all other wines, per gallon, ten cents.
On every gallon of beer, ale or porter in casks, five cents.
On all cyder, beer, ale or porter in bottles, per dozen, twenty cents.
On malt, per bushel, ten cents.
On brown sugars, per pound, one cent.
On loaf sugars, per pound, three cents.
On all other sugars, per pound, one and a half cents.
On coffee, per pound, two and a half cents.
On cocoa, per pound, one cent.
On all candles of tallow, per pound, two cents.
On all candles of wax or spermaceti, per pound, six cents.
On cheese, per pound, four cents.
On soap, per pound, two cents.
On boots, per pair, fifty cents.
On all shoes, slippers or goloshoes made of leather, per pair, seven cents.
On all shoes or slippers made of silk or stuff, per pair, ten cents.

[27]

On cables, for every one hundred and twelve pounds, seventy-five cents.

On tarred cordage, for every one hundred and twelve pounds, seventy-five cents.

On untarred ditto, and yarn, for every one hundred and twelve pounds, ninety cents.

On twine or packthread, for every one hundred and twelve pounds, two hundred cents.

On all steel unwrought, for every one hundred and twelve pounds, fifty-six cents.

On all nails and spikes, per pound, one cent.

On salt, per bushel, six cents.

On manufactured tobacco, per pound, six cents.

On snuff, per pound, ten cents.

On indigo, per pound, sixteen cents.

On wool and cotton cards, per dozen, fifty cents.

On coal, per bushel, two cents.

On pickled fish, per barrel, seventy-five cents.

On dried fish, per quintal, fifty cents.

Specific duties on certain enumerated articles.

On all teas imported from China or India, in ships built in the United States, and belonging to a citizen or citizens thereof, or in ships or vessels built in foreign countries, and on the sixteenth day of May last wholly the property of a citizen or citizens of the United States, and so continuing until the time of importation, as follows:

On bohea tea, per pound, six cents.

On all souchong, or other black teas, per pound, ten cents.

On all hyson teas, per pound, twenty cents.

On all other green teas, per pound, twelve cents.

On teas imported from India or China.

On all teas imported from Europe in ships or vessels built in the United States, and belonging wholly to a citizen or citizens thereof, or in ships or vessels built in foreign countries, and on the sixteenth day of May last wholly the property of a citizen or citizens of the United States, and so continuing until the time of importation, as follows:

On teas imported from Europe.

[28]

On bohea tea, per pound, eight cents.
On all souchong, and other black teas, per pound, thirteen cents.
On all hyson teas, per pound, twenty-six cents.
On all other green teas, per pound, sixteen cents.

On all teas imported in any other manner than as abovementioned, as follows:

On bohea tea, per pound, fifteen cents.
On all souchong, or other black teas, per pound, twenty-two cents.
On all hyson teas, per pound, forty-five cents.
On all other green teas, per pound, twenty-seven cents.

On all other goods imported from India or China, 12½ per centum ad valorem. — On all goods, wares and merchandizes, other than teas, imported from China or India, in ships not built in the United States, and not wholly the property of a citizen or citizens thereof, nor in vessels built in foreign countries, and on the sixteenth day of May last wholly the property of a citizen or citizens of the United States, and so continuing until the time of importation, twelve and a half per centum ad valorem.

On other enumerated articles, ten per centum ad valorem. —
⎱ On all looking-glasses, window and other glass (except black quart bottles)
⎰ On all China, stone and earthen ware,
On gunpowder,
On all paints ground in oil,
On shoe and knee buckles,
On gold and silver lace, and
On gold and silver leaf, ⎱ Ten per centum ad valorem.

On other enumerated articles, seven and an half pr. cent. ad valorem. —
On all blank books,
On all writing, printing or wrapping paper, paper hangings and pasteboard,
On all cabinet wares,
On all buttons,
On all saddles,
On all gloves of leather,
On all hats of beaver, fur, wool, or mixture of either, ⎱ Seven and an half per centum ad valorem.

On all millenary ready made,
On all castings of iron, and upon flit and rolled iron,
On all leather tanned or tawed, and all manufacture of leather, except such as shall be otherwise rated,
On canes, walking sticks and whips,
On cloathing ready made,
On all brushes,
On gold, silver and plated ware, and on jewellery and paste work,
On anchors, and on all wrought tin and pewter ware,
} Seven and an half per centum ad valorem.

On other enumerated articles, leven and an halfpr.cent. ad valorem.

On playing cards, per pack, ten cents.
On every coach, chariot or other four wheel carriage, and on every chaise, solo or other two wheel carriage, or parts thereof, } fifteen per centum ad valorem.

On all other goods, wares and merchandize, five per centum on the value thereof at the time and place of importation, except as follows: salt petre, tin in pigs, tin plates, lead, old pewter, brass, iron and brass wire, copper in plates, wool, cotton, dying woods and dying drugs, raw hides, beaver, and all other furs and deer-skins.

On all other goods, except certain articles, five per cent. on the value at the time & place of importation.

Sec. 2. *And be it further enacted by the authority aforesaid*, That from and after the first day of December, which shall be in the year one thousand seven hundred and ninety, there shall be laid a duty on every one hundred and twelve pounds weight of hemp imported as aforesaid, of sixty cents; and on cotton per pound, three cents.

Duty on hemp and cotton imported after the 1st of Dec. 1790.

Sec. 3. *And be it enacted by the authority aforesaid*, That all the duties paid, or secured to be paid upon any of the goods, wares and merchandizes as aforesaid, except on distilled spirits, other than brandy and geneva, shall be returned or discharged upon

Drawback allowed for the duties on goods exported within 12 months.

E

such of the said goods, wares or merchandizes, as shall within twelve months after payment made, or security given, be exported to any country without the limits of the United States, as settled by the late treaty of peace; except one per centum on the amount of the said duties, in consideration of the expence which shall have accrued by the entry and safe-keeping thereof.

Except one per cent.

Sec. 4. *And be it enacted by the authority aforesaid,* That there shall be allowed and paid on every quintal of dried, and on every barrel of pickled fish, of the fisheries of the United States, and on every barrel of salted provision of the United States, exported to any country without the limits thereof, in lieu of a drawback of the duties imposed on the importation of the salt employed and expended therein, viz.

Allowance in lieu of a drawback on dried & pickled fish and salted provision exported.

On every quintal of dried fish, five cents.
On every barrel of pickled fish, five cents.
On every barrel of salted provision, five cents.

Sec. 5. *And be it further enacted by the authority aforesaid,* That a discount of ten per cent. on all the duties imposed by this act, shall be allowed on such goods, wares and merchandizes, as shall be imported in vessels built in the United States, and which shall be wholly the property of a citizen or citizens thereof, or in vessels built in foreign countries, and on the sixteenth day of May last, wholly the property of a citizen or citizens of the United States, and so continuing until the time of importation.

Discount on the duties for goods imported in vessels of citizens.

Sec. 6. *And be it further enacted by the authority aforesaid,* That this act shall continue and be in force until the first day of June, which shall be in the year of our Lord one thousand seven hundred and ninety-six, and from thence until the end of

Continuance of the act.

the next succeeding session of Congress, which shall be held thereafter, and no longer,

FREDERICK AUGUSTUS MUHLENBERG,
Speaker of the House of Representatives.

JOHN ADAMS, *Vice-President of the United States, and President of the Senate.*

APPROVED, July 4th, 1789.
GEORGE WASHINGTON,
President of the United States.

CHAPTER III.

An ACT *imposing* DUTIES *on* TONNAGE.

Section 1. BE *it enacted by the* SENATE *and* HOUSE *of* REPRESENTATIVES *of the United States of America in Congress assembled,* That the following duties shall be, and are hereby imposed on all ships or vessels entered in the United States, that is to say:

On all ships or vessels built within the said States, and belonging wholly to a citizen or citizens thereof; or not built within the said States, but on the twenty-ninth day of May, one thousand seven hundred and eighty-nine, belonging, and during the time such ships or vessels shall continue to belong wholly to a citizen or citizens thereof, at the rate of six cents per ton. On all ships or vessels hereafter built in the United States, belonging wholly, or in part, to subjects of foreign powers, at the rate of thirty cents per ton. On all other ships or vessels, at the rate of fifty cents per ton.

Tonnage on vessels built in the U. States, or belonging to citizens.

On vessels hereafter built in the U. States, & belonging to foreigners. On all other vessels

Sec. 2. *Provided always, and be it enacted,* That no ship or vessel built within the aforesaid States, and belonging to a citizen or citizens thereof, shall, whilst employed in the coasting trade, or in the fisheries, pay tonnage more than once in any year.

No vessels in the coasting trade to pay tonnage more than once in any year.

Tonnage on vessels of foreigners employed in the coasting trade.

Sec. 3. *And be it further enacted,* That every ship or vessel employed in the transportation of any of the produce or manufactures of the United States, coastwise within the said States, except such ship or vessel be built within the said States, and belong to a citizen or citizens thereof, shall on each entry, pay fifty cents per ton.

Commencement of the act.

Sec. 4. *And be it further enacted,* That this act shall commence and be in force from and after the fifteenth day of August next.

   FREDERICK AUGUSTUS MUHLENBERG,
    Speaker of the House of Representatives.
 JOHN ADAMS, *Vice-President of the United States,*
    and President of the Senate.
 APPROVED, July twentieth, 1789.
   GEORGE WASHINGTON,
    President of the United States.

CHAPTER IV.

An ACT for establishing an Executive Department, to be denominated the DEPARTMENT OF FOREIGN AFFAIRS.

Secretary of foreign affairs, his duty.

Section 1. BE it enacted by the SENATE and HOUSE of REPRESENTATIVES of the United States of America in Congress assembled, That there shall be an executive department, to be denominated the department of foreign affairs, and that there shall be a principal officer therein, to be called the Secretary for the Department of Foreign Affairs, who shall perform and execute such duties as shall from time to time be enjoined on or intrusted to him by the President of the United States, agreeable to the Constitution, relative to correspondences, commissions or instructions to or with public ministers or consuls, from the United States, or to negociations with public ministers from foreign states or princes, or to memorials or other applications from foreign public ministers or other foreigners, or to such other matters respecting foreign affairs, as the President of the United States shall assign to the said department: And furthermore, that the said principal officer shall conduct the business of the said department in such manner as the President of the United States shall from time to time order or instruct.

Sec. 2. *And be it further enacted,* That there shall be in the said department, an inferior officer, to be appointed by the said principal officer, and to be employed therein as he shall deem proper, and to be called the chief clerk in the department of foreign affairs, and who, whenever the said principal officer shall be removed from office by the President of the United States, or in any other case of vacancy, shall, during such vacancy, have the charge and custody of all records, books and papers appertaining to the said department. Principal clerk, his duty.

Sec. 3. *And be it further enacted,* That the said principal officer, and every other person to be appointed or employed in the said department, shall, before he enters on the execution of his office or employment, take an oath or affirmation, well and faithfully to execute the trust committed to him. Oath of office.

Sec. 4. *And be it further enacted,* That the Secretary for the department of foreign affairs, to be appointed in consequence of this act, shall forthwith after his appointment, be entitled to have the custody and charge of all records, books and papers in the office of Secretary for the department of foreign affairs, heretofore established by the United States in Congress assembled. Secretary to take charge of papers, &c. of foreign department.

 FREDERICK AUGUSTUS MUHLENBERG,
  Speaker of the House of Representatives.

JOHN ADAMS, *Vice-President of the United States,*
  and President of the Senate.

 Approved, July 27, 1789.

  GEORGE WASHINGTON,
   President of the United States.

CHAPTER V.

An ACT *to regulate the* COLLECTION *of the* DUTIES *imposed by Law on the* TONNAGE *of* SHIPS *or* VESSELS, *and on* GOODS, WARES *and* MERCHANDIZES *imported into the United States.*

Section 1. BE *it enacted by the* SENATE *and* HOUSE *of* REPRESENTATIVES *of the United States of America in Congress assembled,* That for the due collection of the duties imposed by law on the tonnage of ships and vessels, and on goods, wares and merchandizes imported into the United States, there shall be established and appointed, districts, ports, and officers, in manner following, to wit:

Recital.

The state of NEW-HAMPSHIRE shall be one district, to include the town of Portsmouth as the sole port of entry; and the towns of Newcastle, Dover and Exeter, as ports of delivery only; but all ships or vessels bound to or from either of the said ports of delivery, shall first come to, enter and clear at Portsmouth; and a naval-officer, collector and surveyor for the said district shall be appointed, to reside at Portsmouth.

District and ports in N. Hampshire.

In the state of MASSACHUSETTS shall be twenty districts and ports of entry, to wit: Newburyport, Gloucester, Salem and Beverly, as one port, Marblehead, Boston and Charlestown, as one port, Plymouth, Barnstable, Nantucket, Edgartown, New-Bedford, Dighton, York, Biddeford and Pepperelborough, as one port, Portland and Falmouth, as one port, Bath, Wiscasset, Penobscot, Frenchman's Bay, Machias and Passamaquody. To the district of Newburyport shall be annexed the several towns or landing-places of Almsbury, Salisbury, and Haverhill, which shall be ports of delivery only; and a collector, naval-officer and surveyor for the district shall be appointed, to reside at Newburyport. To the district of Gloucester shall be annexed the town

Districts & ports in Massachusetts.

of Manchester, as a port of delivery only; and a collector and surveyor shall be appointed, to reside at Gloucester. To the district of Salem and Beverly shall be annexed the towns or landing-places of Danvers and Ipswich, as ports of delivery only; and a collector, naval-officer and surveyor for the district shall be appointed, to reside at Salem; and a surveyor to reside at each of the towns of Beverly and Ipswich. To the district of Marblehead shall be annexed the town of Lynn, as a port of delivery only; and a collector for the district shall be appointed, to reside at Marblehead. To the district of Boston and Charlestown shall be annexed the towns or landing-places of Medford, Cohasset, and Hingham, as ports of delivery only; and a collector, naval-officer and surveyor shall be appointed, to reside at Boston. To the district of Plymouth shall be annexed the several towns or landing-places of Scituate, Duxbury and Kingston, as ports of delivery only; and a collector for the district shall be appointed, to reside at Plymouth. To the district of Barnstable shall be annexed the several towns or landing-places of Sandwich, Harwich, Welfleet, Provincetown and Chatham, as ports of delivery only; and a collector for the district shall be appointed, to reside at Barnstable. In the district of Nantucket, the port of Sherbourne shall be the sole port of entry and delivery within the same; and a collector shall be appointed, to reside at Sherbourne. To the district of Edgartown shall be annexed Falmouth, as a port of delivery only; and a collector shall be appointed, to reside at Edgartown. To the district of New-Bedford shall be annexed Westport, Rochester, and Wareham, as ports of delivery only; and a collector for the district shall be appointed, to reside at New-Bedford. To the district of Dighton shall be annexed Swansey and Freetown, as ports of delivery only; and a collector for the district shall be appointed, to re-

Districts & ports in Massachusetts.

Districts & ports in Massachusetts.

side at Dighton. To the district of York shall be annexed Kittery and Berwick, as ports of delivery only; and a collector for the district shall be appointed, to reside at York. To the district of Biddeford and Pepperelborough shall be annexed Scarborough, Wells, Kennebunk, and Cape-Porpoise, as ports of delivery only; and a collector for the district shall be appointed, to reside at Biddeford. To the district of Portland and Falmouth shall be annexed North-Yarmouth and Brunswick, as ports of delivery only; and a collector and surveyor shall be appointed for the district, to reside at Portland. To the district of Bath shall be annexed Hallowell, Pittstown, and Topsham, as ports of delivery only; and a collector for the district shall be appointed, to reside at Bath. To the district of Wiscasset shall be annexed Bristol, Boothbay, and Waldoborough, as ports of delivery only; and a collector for the district shall be appointed, to reside at Wiscasset. To the district of Penobscot shall be annexed Thomaston, Frankfort, Sedgwick-Point, and Deer-Island, as ports of delivery only; and a collector for the district shall be appointed, to reside at Penobscot. To the district of Frenchman's-Bay shall be annexed Union-River, as a port of delivery only, and a collector for the district shall be appointed, to reside at Frenchman's Bay. For each of the districts of Machias and Passamaquody shall be appointed a collector, to reside at the said ports of Machias and Passamaquody respectively. The district of Newburyport shall include all the waters and shores from the state of New-Hampshire, to the north line of Ipswich. The district of Gloucester shall include all the waters and shores in the towns of Gloucester and Manchester. The district of Salem and Beverly shall include all the shores and waters within the towns of Ipswich, Beverly, Salem, and Danvers. The district of Marblehead shall include all the waters and shores within the towns of Marblehead and Lynn. The district of Boston and Charlestown shall include all the waters and shores within the counties of Middlesex and Suffolk. The district of Plymouth shall include all the waters and shores within the county of Plymouth, excepting the towns of Wareham and Rochester. The district of Barnstable shall include all the shores and waters within the county of Barnstable, excepting the town of Falmouth. The district of Nantucket shall include the island of Nantucket. The district of Edgartown shall include all the waters and shores within the county of Duke's-County and the town of Falmouth. The district of New-Bedford shall include all the waters and shores within the towns of New-Bedford, Dartmouth, Westport, Rochester and Wareham, together with all the islands within the county of Bristol. The district of Dighton shall include all the waters and shores on Taunton river, and in the town of Rehoboth; and the collectors of the several districts within that part of the state of Massachusetts, eastward of New-Hampshire, shall agree as soon as may be upon a divisional line between their respective districts, and transmit the same to the Comptroller of the Treasury; and such districts so agreed upon, shall include all the shores, waters and islands within the same.

Districts and ports in Massachusetts.

In the state of CONNECTICUT shall be three districts, to wit: New-London, New-Haven, and Fairfield. The district of New-London shall extend from the east line of the said state of Connecticut to the west line of the town of Killingsworth, and north to the south line of the state of Massachusetts, and shall also include the several towns or landing places of Norwich, Stonington, Groton, Lyme, Saybrook, Haddam, East-Haddam, Middletown, Chatham, Weathersfield, Glastenbury, Hartford, East-Hartford and Killingsworth, as ports of delivery only; New-London to be the sole port of

Districts and ports in Connecticut.

entry; and a collector and surveyor for the district shall be appointed, to reside at New-London, and a surveyor to reside at each of the ports of Stonington and Middletown. The district of New-Haven shall extend from the west line of the district of New-London, westerly to Ousatumnick river; to which shall be annexed the several towns or landing-places of Guilford, Brandford, Milford, and Derby, as ports of delivery only; New-Haven to be the sole port of entry; and a collector and surveyor for the district shall be appointed, to reside at New-Haven. The district of Fairfield shall include all the ports and places in the said state of Connecticut, west of the district of New-Haven, to which shall be annexed the several towns or landing-places of Norwalk, Stratford, Stamford, and Greenwich, as ports of delivery only; Fairfield to be the sole port of entry; and a collector for the district shall be appointed, to reside at Fairfield—And New-London, New-Haven and Fairfield, shall severally be ports of entry.

Districts & ports in N. York.

In the state of NEW-YORK shall be two districts, to wit: Sagg-harbour on Nassau or Long-Island, and the city of New-York, each of which shall be a port of entry. The district of Sagg-harbour shall include all bays, harbours, rivers, and shores, within the two points of land, which are called Oyster-Pond Point, and Montauk Point; and a collector for the district shall be appointed, to reside at Sagg-harbour, which shall be the only place of delivery in the said district. The district of the city of New-York shall include such part of the coasts, rivers, bays and harbours of the said state, not included in the district of Sagg-harbour, and moreover, the several towns or landing places of New-Windsor, Newburgh, Poughkeepsie, Esopus, city of Hudson, Kinderhook, and Albany, as ports of delivery only; and a naval officer, collector and surveyor for the district shall be appointed, to reside at the city of New-York; also two surveyors, one to reside at the city of Albany, and the other at the city of Hudson; and all ships or vessels bound to, or from any port of delivery within the last named district, shall be obliged to come to, and enter or clear out at the city of New-York.

In the state of NEW-JERSEY shall be three districts, to wit: Perth-Amboy, Burlington, and Bridgetown, which shall severally be ports of entry. The district of Perth-Amboy shall comprehend all that part of the state of New-Jersey known by the name of East New-Jersey (that part excepted which is hereafter included in the district of Burlington) together with all the waters thereof, heretofore within the jurisdiction of the said state, in which district the towns or landing places of New-Brunswick, Middletown-Point, Elizabeth-Town and Newark shall be ports of delivery only; and a collector for the district shall be appointed, to reside at Perth-Amboy. The district of Burlington shall comprehend that part of the said state known by the name of West New-Jersey, which lies to the eastward and northward of the county of Gloucester, with all the waters thereof, heretofore within the jurisdiction of the said state, including the river and inlet of Little Egg-harbour, with the waters emptying into the same, and the sea coast, sound, inlets and harbours thereof, from Barnegat inlet to Brigantine inlets, in which district the landing places of Lamberton and Little Egg-harbour shall be ports of delivery only; and a collector shall be appointed for the district, to reside at Burlington, and a surveyor at Little Egg-harbour. The district of Bridgetown shall comprehend the counties of Gloucester, Salem, Cumberland and Cape May (that part of Gloucester county excepted, which is included within the district of Burlington) and all the waters thereof heretofore within the jurisdiction of the said state;

Districts and ports in N. Jersey.

and the town of Salem, Port Elizabeth on Maurice river, and Stillwell's landing on Great Egg-harbour, shall be ports of delivery only; and a collector for the district shall be appointed, to reside at Bridgetown.

<small>District and ports in Pennsylvania.</small> The state of PENNSYLVANIA, shall be one district, and Philadelphia shall be the sole port both of entry and delivery for the same; and a naval-officer, collector and surveyor for the district shall be appointed, to reside at the said port of Philadelphia.

<small>District and ports in Delaware.</small> The state of DELAWARE shall be one district, and the Borough of Wilmington shall be the port of entry, to which shall be annexed Newcastle and Port Penn as ports of delivery only; and a collector for the district shall be appointed, to reside at the said port of Wilmington.

<small>Districts and ports in Maryland.</small> In the state of MARYLAND shall be nine districts, to wit: Baltimore, Chester, Oxford, Vienna, Snow-Hill, Annapolis, Nottingham, Nanjemoy, and George-Town. The district of Baltimore shall include Patapsco, Susquehannah and Elk rivers, and all the waters and shores on the west side of Chesapeake Bay, from the mouth of Magetty river to the south side of Elk river, inclusive, in which Havre de Grace and Elkton shall be ports of delivery only; and a naval-officer, collector and surveyor shall be appointed for the said district, to reside at the town of Baltimore, which shall be the sole port of entry. The district of Chester shall include Chester river, and all the waters and shores on the eastern side of Chesapeake Bay, from the south side of Elk river to the north side of the eastern bay and Wye river, exclusive, in which George-Town on Saffafras river shall be a port of delivery only; and a collector for the district shall be appointed, to reside at Chester, which shall be the sole port of entry. The district of Oxford shall

include all the waters and shores on the eastern side of Chesapeake Bay, from the north side of Wye river and the eastern bay, to the south side of Choptank river, inclusive, and Cambridge shall be a port of delivery only; and a collector for the district shall be appointed, to reside at Oxford, which shall be the sole port of entry. The district of Vienna shall include all the waters and shores on the eastern side of Chesapeake Bay, from the south side of Choptank river to the south side of Wicomico river, inclusive, and Salisbury shall be a port of delivery only; and a collector for the district shall be appointed, to reside at Vienna, which shall be the sole port of entry. The district of Snow-Hill shall include all the waters and shores on the sea coast, from the north line of Virginia to the south line of Delaware, together with all the waters and shores on the eastern side of Chesapeake Bay, from the south side of Wicomico river to the south side of Pocomoke river, inclusive, so far as the jurisdiction of the said state of Maryland extends, to which Sinnepuxent shall be a port of delivery for West-India produce only; and a collector for the district shall be appointed, to reside at Snow-Hill, which shall be the sole port of entry. The district of Annapolis shall include Magetty river, and all the waters and shores from thence to Drum-Point, on Patuxent river; and a collector for the district shall be appointed, to reside at Annapolis, which shall be the sole port of entry and delivery for the same. The district of Nottingham shall include all the waters and shores on the west side of Chesapeake Bay to Drum-Point, on the river Patuxent, together with the said river, and all the navigable waters emptying into the same, to which Benedict, Lower Marlborough, Town Creek, and Silvey's landing, shall be annexed as ports of delivery only; a collector for the district shall be appointed, to reside at Nottingham; and a surveyor at Town-Creek;

Districts and ports in Maryland.

<small>Districts and ports in Maryland.</small> and Nottingham shall be the sole port of entry. The district of Nanjemoy shall include all the waters of Potowmac river, within the jurisdiction of the state of Maryland, from Point Look-out to Pomonkey creek, inclusive, to which Saint Mary's shall be annexed as a port of delivery only; and a collector for the district shall be appointed, to reside at Nanjemoy; also a surveyor to reside at Saint Mary's, and Nanjemoy shall be the sole port of entry. The district of George-Town shall include all the waters and shores from Pomonkey creek, on the north side of Potowmac river, to the head of the navigable waters of the said river, within the jurisdiction of the state of Maryland, to which Digges's landing and Carrollsburg shall be annexed as ports of delivery only; and a collector for the district shall be appointed, to reside at George-Town, which shall be the sole port of entry.

<small>Districts and ports in Virginia.</small> In the state of VIRGINIA shall be twelve districts, to wit: Hampton as one port; Norfolk and Portsmouth as one port; Bermuda-Hundred and City-Point as one port; York-Town, Tappahannock, Yeocomico river, including Kinsale, Dumfries, including Newport, Alexandria, Folly-Landing, Cherry-Stone, South-Quay, and Louisville; the authority of the officers at Hampton shall extend over all the waters, shores, bays, harbours, and inlets, between the south side of the mouth of York river, along the west shore of Chesapeake-Bay to Hampton, and thence up James river to the west side of Chickahominy river; and a collector shall be appointed, to reside at Hampton, which shall be the sole port of entry. To the district of Norfolk and Portsmouth shall be annexed Suffolk, and Smithfield as ports of delivery only; and the authority of the officers of the said district shall extend over all the waters, shores, bays, harbours, and inlets, comprehended within a line drawn from Cape-Henry to the mouth of James river,

and thence up James river to Jordon's-Point, and up Elizabeth river to the highest tide water thereof; and Norfolk and Portsmouth shall be the sole port of entry; and a collector, naval-officer and surveyor for the district shall be appointed, to reside at Norfolk; also a surveyor to reside at each of the ports of Suffolk and Smithfield. To the district of Bermuda-Hundred, or City-Point, shall be annexed Richmond, Petersburg and Manchester, as ports of delivery only; and a collector and surveyor shall be appointed, to reside at Bermuda-Hundred, or City-Point, which shall be the sole port of entry; also a surveyor for Petersburg, to reside thereat, and a surveyor for Richmond and Manchester, to reside at Richmond; and the authority of the officers of the said district shall extend over all the waters, shores, bays, harbours and inlets, comprehended between Jordon's-Point and the highest tide water on James and Appomattox rivers. To the district of York-Town shall be annexed Westpoint and Cumberland, as ports of delivery only; and a collector for the district shall be appointed, to reside at York-Town, which shall be the sole port of entry; also a surveyor for the two ports of delivery, to reside at Westpoint; and the authority of the officers of the said district shall extend over all the waters, shores, bays, harbours and inlets, comprehended between the point forming the south shore of the mouth of Rappahannock river, and the point forming the south shore of the mouth of York river, and thence up the said river to Westpoint, and thence up Pamunkey and Mattapony rivers, to the highest navigable waters thereof. To the district of Tappahannock shall be annexed Urbanna, Port-Royal, Fredericksburg and Falmouth, as ports of delivery only; and a collector for the district shall be appointed, to reside at Tappahannock, which shall be the sole port of entry; also a surveyor for each of the ports of Ur-

<small>Districts and ports in Virginia.</small>

Districts and ports in Virginia.

banna, Port-Royal, and Fredericksburg, and the authority of the officers of the said district shall extend over all the waters, shores, bays, harbours and inlets, comprehended between Smith's-Point, at the mouth of Potowmac, and the point forming the south shore of the mouth of Rappahannock river, and thence up the last mentioned river to the highest tide water thereof. The district of Yeocomico river, including Kinsale, shall extend from Smith's-Point on the south side of Potowmac river, to Boyd's-Hole on the same river, including all the waters, shores, bays, rivers, creeks, harbours and inlets, along the south shore of Potowmac river to Boyd's-Hole aforesaid; and Yeocomico, including Kinsale, shall be the sole port of entry; and a collector shall be appointed, to reside on Yeocomico river. The district of Dumfries, including Newport, shall extend from Boyd's-Hole to Cockpit-Point on the south side of Potowmac river; and a collector shall be appointed, to reside at Dumfries, which shall be the sole port of entry; and the authority of the officers of this district shall extend over all the waters, shores, bays, harbours and inlets comprehended between Boyd's-Hole and Cockpit-Point aforesaid. For the district of Alexandria shall be appointed a collector and surveyor, to reside at Alexandria, which shall be the sole port of entry; and the authority of the officers of the said district shall extend over all the waters, shores, bays, harbours and inlets on the south side of the river Potowmac, from the last mentioned Cockpit-Point, to the highest tide water of the said river. For the district of Folly-Landing shall be appointed a collector, who shall reside at Accomack Court-House, and whose authority shall extend over all the waters, shores, bays, harbours and inlets of the county of Accomack. For the district of Cherry-Stone shall be appointed a collector, to reside at Cherry-Stone, whose authority shall extend over all the waters, shores, bays, harbours and inlets comprehended within Northampton county. For the district of South-Quay a collector shall be appointed, to reside thereat, whose authority shall extend over all the waters, shores, bays, harbours and inlets in that part of Virginia, comprehended within the limits of the said state. For the district of Louisville a collector shall be appointed, to reside thereat, whose authority shall extend over all waters, shores and inlets, included between the rapids and the mouth of Ohio river, on the south-east side thereof.

Districts and ports in Virginia.

In the state of SOUTH-CAROLINA shall be three districts, to wit: Georgetown, Charleston and Beaufort, each of which shall be a port of entry. The district of Georgetown shall include the shores, inlets and rivers, from the boundary of North-Carolina to the point of Cape-Roman. The district of Charleston shall include all the shores, inlets and rivers, from Cape-Roman to Combahee river, inclusive; and the district of Beaufort shall include the shores, inlets and rivers from Combahee river to Back river in Georgia, comprehending also the shores, inlets and harbours, formed by the different bars and sea islands, lying within each district respectively; at the port of Charleston shall be a collector, naval-officer and surveyor, and a collector at each of the other ports.

Districts and ports in South-Carolina.

In the state of GEORGIA shall be four districts, to wit: Savannah, Sunbury, Brunswick, and Saint Mary's, each of which shall be a port of entry. The district of Savannah shall include Savannah river, Great and Little Ogeechee rivers, with the other harbours, creeks and rivers, formed by the inlets of Tybee, Little Tybee, Warsaw and Ossabaw, north of the island of Ossabaw; and a naval-officer, collector and surveyor, for the said district shall be appointed, to reside at Savannah. The district of Sunbury shall include the Medway, North and

Districts and ports in Georgia.

[46]

<small>District and ports in Georgia.</small> South Newport, and Sapelo rivers, with the harbours, creeks and rivers, formed by the inlets of Saint Catharine's, south of Ossabaw and Sapelo; and a collector for the district shall be appointed, to reside at Sunbury. The district of Brunswick shall include the Alatamaha, Frederica, and Turtle rivers, with the other harbours, creeks and rivers, formed by the inlets of Doboy south of Sapelo, Alatamaha, and Saint Simons, north of the south point of Jekyl island; Frederica shall be a port of delivery only; and a collector for the said district shall be appointed, to reside at Brunswick; the district of Saint Mary's shall include Great Setilla, Little Setilla, Crooked river, and Saint Mary's river, with the harbours, creeks and rivers, formed by the inlets of Saint Andrews and Amelia sounds; and a collector for the said district shall be appointed, to reside at Saint Mary's. And in each district it shall be lawful for the collector to grant a permit to unlade at any port or place within the district, and to appoint or put on board any ship or vessel for which a permit is granted, one or more searchers or inspectors, as may be necessary for the security of the revenue.

<small>Ports of entry to be ports of delivery, also.</small> Sec. 2. *And be it further enacted,* That every port of entry established by this act, shall be a port of delivery also: *Provided always,* That no ship or vessel not wholly belonging to a citizen or citizens of the United States, shall be admitted to unload at any port or place except the following, to <small>Ports of delivery to which foreign vessels are restricted.</small> wit: Portsmouth, in the State of New-Hampshire, Portland, Falmouth, Dighton, Salem, Gloucester, Newburyport, Marblehead, Sherbourne, Boston, Plymouth, Wiscasset, Machias, and Penobscot, in the State of Massachusetts; New-London or New-Haven, in the State of Connecticut; New-York; Perth-Amboy or Burlington, in the State of New-Jersey; Philadelphia; Wilmington, New-Castle and Port-Penn, in the State of Delaware;

Baltimore, Annapolis, Vienna, Oxford, George-Town on Potowmac, Chester-Town, Town Creek, Nottingham, Nanjemoy, Digges's-landing, Snow-Hill and Carrollsburg, in the State of Maryland; Alexandria, Kinsale, Newport, Tappahannock, Port-Royal, Fredericksburgh, Urbanna, York-Town, West-Point, Hampton, Bermuda-Hundred, City-Point, Rocket's-landing, Norfolk or Portsmouth, in the State of Virginia; Charleston, George-Town or Beaufort, in the State of South-Carolina; or in either of the districts of Savannah, Sunbury, Brunswick or Saint Mary's, in the State of Georgia: nor shall any ship or vessel arriving from the Cape of Good Hope, or from any place beyond the same, be admitted to enter at any other than the following ports, to wit: Portsmouth, in the State of New-Hampshire; Boston, Newburyport, Salem, Gloucester, Portland or Falmouth, in the State of Massachusetts; New-London or New-Haven, in the State of Connecticut; New-York; Perth-Amboy; Philadelphia; Wilmington, in the State of Delaware; Baltimore-Town, Annapolis, or George-Town, in the State of Maryland; Alexandria, Norfolk, or Portsmouth, in the State of Virginia; Charleston, George-Town, or Beaufort, in the State of South-Carolina; Sunbury, or Savannah, in the State of Georgia: *Provided*, That nothing herein contained shall be construed to prevent the master or commander of any ship or vessel, from making entry with the collector of any port or district in which such ship or vessel may be owned, or from whence she may have sailed on such a voyage.

Ports of entry to which vessels arriving from the Cape of Good Hope or beyond it are restricted.

Sec. 3. *And be it further enacted*, That the master or commander of every ship or vessel bound to a port of delivery only, in any of the following districts, to wit: Portland and Falmouth, Bath, Newburyport, New-London, (except the port of Stonington in the said district) Norfolk and Ports-

Ports of delivery to which vessels bound shall first come to at the port of entry.

mouth, Bermuda-Hundred and City-Point, York-Town or Tappahannock (except the port of Urbanna in the said district) shall first come to at the port of entry of such district, with his ship or vessel, and there make entry, deliver a manifest of her cargo, and pay, or secure to be paid, all legal duties, tonnage, port fees and charges, in manner by this act provided, before such ship or vessel shall proceed to her port of delivery; and that any ship or vessel bound to a port of delivery in any other district not under like restrictions by this act, or to either of the ports of Stonington, or Urbanna, may first proceed to her port of delivery, and then make legal entry within the time by this act limited.

Districts to which vessels bound shall not pass certain ports without delivering a manifest.

Sec. 4. *And be it further enacted*, That the master or commander of every ship or vessel, if bound to the district of Nottingham, shall, before he pass by the port of Town-Creek, and immediately after his arrival, deposit with the surveyor of the said port, a true manifest of the cargo on board such ship or vessel; if bound to any district on the Potowmack, shall, before he pass by the rivers Saint Mary's and Yeocomico, and immediately after his arrival, deposit with the surveyor at Saint Mary's, or the collector at Yeocomico, as may be most convenient, a true manifest of the cargo on board such ship or vessel, including a declaration of the port at which the same is to be entered; if bound to the district of Tappahannock, shall, before he pass by the port of Urbanna, and immediately after his arrival, deposit with the surveyor for that port, a like manifest; and if bound to the district of Bermuda-hundred or City-point, shall, before he pass by Elizabeth river, and immediately after his arrival, deposit with the collector of the port of Norfolk and Portsmouth, or with the collector for the port of Hampton, a like manifest; and the said surveyors and collectors respectively, shall, after registering the manifests, transmit the fame duly certified to have been fo depofited to the officer with whom the entries are to be made, without which certificate no fuch entry fhall be received.

Sec. 5. *And be it further enacted,* That the duties of the refpective officers to be appointed by virtue of this act, fhall be as follows: At fuch of the ports to which there fhall be appointed a collector, naval-officer and furveyor, it fhall be the duty of the collector to receive all reports, manifefts and documents made or exhibited to him by the mafter or commander of any fhip or veffel, conformably to the regulations prefcribed by this act, to make due entry and record in books to be kept for that purpofe, all fuch manifefts and the packages, marks and numbers contained therein; to receive the entry of all fhips and veffels, and of all the goods, wares and merchandize imported in fuch fhips or veffels, together with the original invoices thereof; to eftimate the duties payable thereon, and to endorfe the fame on each entry; to receive all monies paid for duties, and to take all bonds for fecuring the payment of duties; to grant all permits for the unlading and delivery of goods, to employ proper perfons as weighers, gaugers, meafurers and infpectors at the feveral ports within his diftrict, together with fuch perfons as fhall be neceffary to ferve in the boats which may be provided for fecuring the collection of the revenue, to provide at the public expence, and with the approbation of the principal officer of the treafury department, ftore houfes for the fafe keeping of goods, together with fuch fcales, weights and meafures as fhall be deemed neceffary, and to perform all other duties which fhall be affigned to him by law. It fhall be the duty of the naval-officer to receive copies of all manifefts, to eftimate and record the duties on each entry made with the collector, and to correct any error made

Duties of the collector.

Naval-officer and furveyor.

therein, before a permit to unlade or deliver shall be granted; to countersign all permits and clearances granted by the collector. It shall be the duty of the surveyor to superintend and direct all inspectors, weighers, measurers and gaugers within his district, and the employment of the boats which may be provided for securing the collection of the revenue; to go on board ships or vessels arriving within his district, or to put on board one or more inspectors, to ascertain by an hydrometer, what distilled spirits shall be of Jamaica proof, rating all distilled spirits which shall be of the proof of twenty-four degrees as of Jamaica proof, and to examine whether the goods imported are conformable to the entries thereof; and the said surveyors shall in all cases be subject to the controul of the collector and naval officer.

<small>Collector may appoint a deputy.</small>

Sec. 6. *And be it further enacted*, That every collector appointed in virtue of this act, in case of his necessary absence, sickness, or inability to execute the duties of his office, may appoint a deputy, duly authorized under his hand and seal, to execute and perform on his behalf, all and singular the powers, functions and duties of collector of the district to which he the said principal is attached, who shall be answerable for the neglect of duty, or other mal-conduct of his said deputy in the execution of the office.

<small>Duties of a deputy collector.</small>

Sec. 7. *And be it further enacted*, That in case of the disability or death of any collector, the duties and authorities vested in him by this act shall devolve on his deputy, if any such hath been appointed (for whose conduct the estate of such disabled or deceased collector shall be liable) and the said deputy shall exercise the authority and perform all the duties, until a successor shall be appointed. But in cases where no deputy is appointed, the authorities and duties of the disabled or deceased collector, shall devolve upon the naval officer of the

same district, until a successor duly authorised and sworn, shall enter upon the execution of the duties of the said office.

Sec. 8. *And be it further enacted,* That at such of the ports established by this act, to which a collector and surveyor only are assigned, the said collector shall execute all the duties herein required to be done by the collector and naval-officer at other ports. That at such ports to which a collector only is assigned, such collector shall possess all the powers, and execute as far as may be, all the duties prescribed to a collector, naval-officer, and surveyor, at the ports where such officers are established; that at such ports of delivery only, to which a surveyor is assigned, it shall be his duty to receive and record the copies of all manifests transmitted to him by the collector; to enter and record all permits granted by such collector, distinguishing the gauge, weight, measure and quality of the goods specified therein; to take care that no goods be unladen or delivered from any ship or vessel without such permit; and to perform all other duties required to be done by a surveyor: That at such ports of delivery only, to which no surveyor is assigned, it shall be the duty of the collector of the district to attend the unlading and delivery of goods, or in cases of necessity, to employ a proper person or persons for that purpose, who shall possess the power, and be entitled to the like compensation allowed to inspectors during the time they are employed. Every collector, naval-officer, and surveyor, shall attend in person at the port or district for which he is appointed, and before he enters on the execution of his office, shall take an oath or affirmation in the form following, to wit:—" I ——— ———, do so-
" lemnly swear or affirm (as the case may be)
" that I will truly and faithfully execute and per-
" form all the duties of a ——— of the port or
" district of ——— according to law, and the best

Farther duties of collector and surveyor.

"of my skill and ability." The said oath or affirmation shall be administered by any justice of the peace, and a certificate thereof, under the hand and seal of such justice, transmitted within three months thereafter to the comptroller of the treasury: Any collector, naval-officer or surveyor, failing herein, shall forfeit and pay two hundred dollars, recoverable with costs in any court having cognizance thereof, to the use of the informer. And no weigher, gauger, measurer or inspector, shall execute the duties of his office, until he shall have taken the above oath or affirmation.

Collectors, naval officers and surveyors to keep books.

Sec. 9. *And be it further enacted,* That the collectors, naval-officers and surveyors to be appointed by virtue of this act, shall respectively keep fair and true accounts of all their transactions relative to their duty as officers of the customs, in such manner and form as may be directed by the proper department, or officer appointed by law to superintend the revenue of the United States; and shall at all times submit their books, papers and accounts, to the inspection of such persons as may be appointed for that purpose: And the collectors of the different ports shall at all times pay to the order of the officer who shall be authorised to direct the same, the whole of the monies which they may respectively receive by virtue of this act (such monies as they are otherwise by this act directed to pay, only excepted) and shall also, once in every three months, or oftner if they shall be required, transmit their accounts for settlement to the department or officer before mentioned.

Collectors to pay all monies received, and settle their accounts every three months.

Masters of vessels from for'n ports to deliver 2 manifests to any officer who shall first go on board.

Sec. 10. *And be it further enacted,* That every master or other person having or taking the charge or command of any ship or vessel, bound to any port of the United States, from any foreign port or place, shall deliver upon demand, to any officer or other person lawfully authorised, who shall first come on board his ship or vessel, two manifests, figned by the faid mafter or perfon having command, and fpecifying in words (and not in figures) a true account of the loading which fuch fhip or veffel had on board at the port from which fhe laft failed, and at the time of her failing, or at any time fince, the packages, marks and numbers, and noting thereon to what port in the United States fuch fhip or veffel is bound, and the name or names of the perfon or perfons to whom the goods are configned, or in cafes where the goods are fhipped to order, the names of the fhippers, noting the goods configned to their order. One of which manifefts, fuch officer, or other perfon fhall fign, and return to the mafter or other perfon having the charge of fuch fhip or veffel, certifying thereon as nearly as may be, the time when the fame was produced, and that a like manifeft was delivered to him; and fhall tranfmit the other manifeft to the collector of the diftrict to which fuch fhip or veffel is bound.

Sec. 11. *And be it further enacted*, That the mafter or other perfon, having the charge or command of any fhip or veffel (fhips and veffels of war excepted) coming into, or arriving in any of the ports or diftricts of the United States, or in any of the creeks or harbours thereof, fhall, within forty-eight hours after fuch arrival, repair to the office of the collector of the diftrict where fuch veffel fhall fo arrive, and fhall report to the faid collector, the place from whence he laft failed, with the name and burthen of his fhip or veffel, and fhall deliver to fuch collector, two manifefts, agreeably to the directions of this act, unlefs he fhall before have delivered one manifeft to fome officer, or other perfon lawfully authorifed in manner as herein before is required; in which cafe he fhall deliver the manifeft certified as aforefaid, together with fuch documents as are ufually furnifhed in the port from whence they came, and fhall take and fubfcribe an

To make entry within 48 hours, & fwear to his manifeft

oath or affirmation, before the collector or other proper officer, which oath or affirmation, he or they are authorifed and required to adminifter, and fhall be in the words following, to wit: "I, ———, do folemnly fwear or affirm (as the cafe may be) that this is, to the beft of my knowledge and belief, a juft and true manifeft of all the goods, wares and merchandize, on board the ———, at the port from which fhe laft failed, at the time of her failing, or at any time fince, and of which vessel I am at prefent mafter." And if the maf-

Penalty on refufal or neglect.

ter or other perfon having charge or command of any fuch fhip or veffel, fhall refufe or neglect to make entry, or deliver his manifefts and documents, purfuant to the directions of this act, or to take the oath or affirmation herein prefcribed, he fhall forfeit and pay five hundred dollars for each refufal or neglect.

Penalty on mafters and others permitting goods to be unladen, unlefs in open day, & with a permit.

Sec. 12. *And be it further enacted*, That no goods, wares or merchandize fhall be unladen or delivered, from any fhip or veffel, but in open day, or without a permit from the collector for that purpofe; and if the mafter or commander of any fhip or veffel fhall fuffer or permit the fame, fuch mafter and commander, and every other perfon who fhall be aiding or affifting in landing, removing, houfing, or otherwife fecuring the fame, fhall forfeit and pay the fum of four hundred dollars for every offence; fhall moreover be difabled from holding any office of truft or profit under the United States, for a term not exceeding feven years; and it fhall be the duty of the collector of the diftrict, to advertife the names of all fuch perfons in the public gazette of the ftate in which he refides, within twenty days

The goods to be forfeited.

after each refpective conviction. And all goods, wares and merchandize fo landed or difcharged, fhall become forfeited, and may be feized by any officer of the cuftoms; and where the value thereof fhall amount to four hundred dollars, the veffel, tackle, apparel and furniture, shall be subject to like forfeiture and seizure: *Provided always,* That if any ship or vessel compelled by distress of weather, or other sufficient cause, shall put into any port or place of the United States, other than that to which she was actually destined, the master or other person having command, shall within forty-eight hours next after his arrival, make report and deliver a true manifest of his cargo to the collector of the port or district; and moreover shall within twenty-four hours, make protest in the usual form before a notary public or justice of the peace, of the cause and circumstances of such distress; and if it shall appear to the collector, that there is a necessity for unloading such ship or vessel, he shall grant permission, and appoint a proper officer to attend the unloading thereof; and all goods, wares and merchandize so unladen, shall be stored under the direction, and subject to the safe keeping of such collector; but if any part thereof shall be of a perishable nature, or it may be necessary to make sale of any part thereof to defray the expences of such vessel or cargo, the said collector shall grant a licence to the master, commander or owner, to dispose of so much thereof as are perishable, or shall be necessary to defray such expences: *Provided,* That the duties thereon be first paid or secured: *And provided also,* That such necessity be made appear by the wardens of the port, or other persons legally authorised to certify the same, and where there are no such persons, by the affidavit of two reputable citizens of the neighbourhood, best acquainted with matters of that kind.

Ships or vessels compelled by distress of weather, to make entry and protest.

Collector may grant a permit to unload and sell perishable goods, or sufficient to defray expences;

the duties being first paid or secured.

Sec. 13. *And be it further enacted,* That every person having goods, wares or merchandize, in any ship or vessel, which shall arrive at any port of entry, or of delivery only, shall make entry with the collector of the port or district, where the same shall arrive, of all such goods, wares and merchandize,

Owner or consignee of goods imported to make entry,

specifying the number of packages, and the marks, numbers and contents of each (or if in bulk, the quantity and quality) together with an account of the nett prime coſt thereof; and ſhall moreover produce to the collector, the original invoice or in- and take an voices, together with the bills of loading: And the oath to the truth there- of. ſaid collector ſhall eſtimate and endorſe the duties on the ſaid entry, the party making ſuch entry taking an oath or affirmation, that it contains the whole of the goods, wares and merchandize im- ported by him, or to him conſigned in ſuch ſhip or veſſel, which ſhall then have come to his know- ledge, and that the ſaid invoice contains to the beſt of his knowledge and belief, the nett prime coſt thereof, and that if he ſhall afterwards diſcover any other, or greater quantity than is contained in ſuch entry, he will make due report and entry thereof: And the ſaid oath or affirmation ſhall be adminiſtered by the collector, and the entry ſhall be ſubſcribed by the perſon making the ſame. *Pro- vided*, That in all caſes where the party making entry ſhall reſide ten miles or upwards from ſuch port, the affidavit or affirmation of ſuch party, ta- ken before a juſtice of the peace, and by him en- dorſed on the original invoices, ſhall be as effec- tual as if adminiſtered and endorſed by the collec- tor.

All entries to be exa- mined and counter- ſigned by the naval- officer.

Sec. 14. *And be it further enacted*, That all ſuch entries ſo authenticated by the collector, toge- ther with a copy of the ſame made out by the par- ty, ſhall, before any permit is granted for the land- ing of any goods, wares or merchandize therein contained, be examined by the naval-officer (where ſuch officer is eſtabliſhed) who ſhall counterſign the ſame, and retaining one, ſhall return the other certified to the party, together with the bills of la- ding, and invoice or invoices; and on ſuch certi- fied entries being returned to the collector, and the duties thereon paid or ſecured to be paid, he shall grant a permit for the unlading and landing the goods, wares and merchandize therein mentioned. And at such ports for which no naval-officer is appointed, the collector shall grant like permits for the unlading and landing of all such goods as shall be so entered, and the duties thereof paid or secured.

Sec. 15. *And be it further enacted*, That it shall and may be lawful for the collector, naval-officer and surveyor, of any port of entry or delivery, at which any ship or vessel may arrive, to put on board such ship or vessel one or more inspectors, who shall make known to the person having charge of such ship or vessel, the duties he is to perform by virtue of this act; and such inspector shall suffer no goods, wares or merchandize, to be delivered without a permit from the proper officer, authorising the same; and shall enter in a book to be by him kept for that purpose, the contents of each permit, specifying the marks and numbers of each package, and a description thereof, with the name of the person to whom such permit was granted; and if at the expiration of fifteen working days after such ship or vessel shall begin to unload her cargo, there shall be found on board, any goods, wares or merchandize, the said inspector shall take possession thereof, and deliver them to the collector of the district, or to such person as he shall authorise or appoint on his behalf to receive the said goods, taking his receipt for the same, and giving a certificate to the person having command, describing the packages, and their marks and numbers, so taken: And as soon as any ship or vessel is entirely unladen, he shall with the collector and naval-officer, compare the account and entries he has made of the goods unladen from such ship or vessel, with the manifest delivered to the collector, and if it appears that there are more goods than are specified in the said manifest, the same shall be

Inspectors to be appointed.

Their duty.

[58]

<small>Infpectors duty.</small>

endorfed thereon, with a defcription of the packages, their marks and numbers, or of fuch goods as may be in bulk, and the fame fhall be fubfcribed by fuch infpector, who is hereby directed to remain on board the faid fhip or veffel until fhe is difcharged : *Provided always,* That the faid limitation of fifteen days fhall not extend to veffels laden with falt or coal, but if the mafter or owner of fuch veffels require longer time to difcharge their cargoes, the wages of the infpector for every day's attendance, exceeding the faid fifteen days, fhall be paid by the mafter or owner. And if any goods, wares or merchandize, fubject to duty, fhall be removed from the wharf or place where the fame may be landed, before they fhall be weighed, or gauged (as the cafe may be) or without the confent of the collector, or other proper officer, all fuch goods, wares and merchandize, fo removed, fhall be forfeited. All goods delivered to the collector in manner aforefaid, fhall be kept at the charge and rifque of the owner, for a term not exceeding nine months ; and if within that time no claim be made for the fame, an appraifement thereof fhall be made by two or more reputable merchants, and lodged with the collector, who fhall fell the fame at public auction, and pay the proceeds, retaining the duties and charges thereon, into the treafury of the United States, there to remain for the ufe of the owner, who fhall upon due proof of his property, be entitled to receive the fame ; and the receipt or certificate of the collector, fhall exonerate the mafter or commander from all claim of the owner. *Provided,* That where entry fhall have been duly made of fuch goods, the fame fhall not be appraifed ; and that where fuch goods are of a perifhable nature, they fhall be fold forthwith.

Sec. 16. *And be it further enacted,* That if any goods, wares or merchandize, on which duties are payable, fhall receive damage during the voyage, or shall not be accompanied with the original invoice of their cost, it shall be lawful for the collector to appoint one merchant, and the owner or consignee another, who being sworn or affirmed by the collector well and truly to appraise such goods, shall value them accordingly, and the duties upon such goods shall be estimated according to such valuation; and if any package, or any goods stowed in bulk, which shall have been entered as is herein before directed, shall not be duly delivered, or if any of the packages so entered shall not agree with the manifest, or if the manifest shall not agree with the delivery, in every such case the person having command shall forfeit and pay the sum of two hundred dollars, unless it shall appear that such disagreement was occasioned by unavoidable necessity or accident, and not with intention to defraud the revenue. *Goods damaged on a voyage, or not accompanied with invoices to be appraised.*

Sec. 17. *And be it further enacted,* That the ad valorem rates of duty upon goods, wares and merchandize, at the place of importation, shall be estimated by adding twenty per cent. to the actual cost thereof, if imported from the Cape of Good-Hope, or from any place beyond the same; and ten per cent. on the actual cost thereof, if imported from any other place or country, exclusive of all charges. *Rule for estimating the ad valorem rates of duty, at the place of importation.*

Sec. 18. *And be it further enacted,* That all foreign coins and currencies shall be estimated according to the following rates; each pound sterling of Great-Britain at four dollars, forty-four cents; each livre tournois of France at eighteen cents and an half; each florin or guilder of the United Netherlands at thirty-nine cents; each mark banco of Hamburgh at thirty-three cents and one third; each rix dollar of Denmark at one hundred cents; each rix dollar of Sweden at one hundred cents; each ruble of Russia at one hundred cents; each real plate of Spain at ten cents; each milree of Portugal at one dollar and twenty-four cents; each *Rates of foreign coin and currencies.*

pound sterling of Ireland at four dollars ten cents; each tale of China at one dollar forty-eight cents; each pagoda of India at one dollar ninety-four cents; each rupee of Bengal at fifty-five cents and a half; and all other denominations of money in value as near as may be to the said rates; and the invoices of all importations shall be made out in the currency of the place or country from whence the importation shall be made, and not otherwise.

Invoices to be in currency the of place from whence the importation comes.

Duties, how to be paid or secured.

Sec. 19. *And be it further enacted,* That all duties on goods, wares and merchandize imported, shall be paid by the importer, before a permit shall be granted for landing the same, unless the amount of such duties shall exceed fifty dollars, in which case it shall be at the option of the party making entry, to secure the same by bond, with one or more sufficient sureties, to be approved of by the collector, and made payable as followeth, to wit: For the duties upon all articles of West-India produce, within four months; for the duties upon all Madeira wines, within twelve months; and for the duties upon all other goods, within six months; but in any case the party making entry shall be at liberty to deposit with the collector any part of the goods, upon which such duties shall arise, of double the value in the judgment of the collector to secure the payment of the duties with the charges, which deposit the collector shall accept in lieu of such bond and security, and shall safely keep the goods so deposited, at the expence and risque of the party, for the term for which such bond would have been given, at the expiration whereof, unless the said deposit shall have been redeemed by the payment of the duties, the said goods shall be sold at public sale, and as much as shall be necessary applied to the payment of the said duties, and the residue, after deducting the charges which have accrued, shall be paid to the owner or owners of such goods. *Provided always,* That where the amount of duties shall exceed fifty dollars, a discount shall be allowed for prompt payment, after the rate of ten per centum per annum on the amount of such excess: *And provided also,* That no person whose bond for the payment of duties is due and unsatisfied, shall be allowed a future credit with the collector, until such bond shall be fully paid or discharged.

Sec. 20. *And be it further enacted,* That all the duties imposed by law on the tonnage of any ship or vessel, shall be paid to the collector, within ten days after entry made, and before such ship or vessel shall be permitted to clear out; the register of which ship or vessel at the time of entry, shall be lodged in the office of the collector, and there remain until such clearance. Duties on tonnage to be paid within ten days, & before clearance.

Sec. 21. *And be it further enacted,* That where any bond for the payment of duties shall not be satisfied on the day it became due, the collector shall prosecute for the recovery of the money due thereon, by action or suit at law, in the proper court, having cognizance therein; and in all cases of insolvency, or where any estate in the hands of executors or administrators, shall be insufficient to pay all the debts due from the deceased, the debt due to the United States on any such bonds shall be first satisfied. Bond for duties, how to be prosecuted.

Sec. 22. *And be it further enacted,* That when it shall appear that any goods, wares or merchandize of which entry shall have been made, in the office of a collector, are not invoiced, according to the actual cost thereof at the place of exportation, and that the difference was made with design to defraud the revenue, all such goods, wares or merchandize, or the value thereof to be recovered of the person making entry, shall be forfeited; and in any such case, or where the collector is suspicious of fraud, and that any such goods, Goods entered & not truly invoiced, to be forfeited.

wares or merchandize, are not invoiced at a sum equal to that for which they have usually sold, in the place or country from whence they were imported, it shall be the duty of such collector to take the said goods, wares and merchandize into his possession, and retain the same at the risque and expence of the owner or consignee thereof, until their value, at the time and place of importation, according to the principles for estimating the same, established by this act, shall be ascertained by two reputable merchants, mutually chosen by the said collector, and owner or consignee, and the duties arising upon such valuation shall be first paid, or secured to be paid, as required by this act in other cases of importation.

<small>How to be ascertained.</small>

<small>Collector or other officer suspecting fraud, may open & examine packages.</small>

Sec. 23. *And be it further enacted*, That it shall be lawful for the collector, or other officer of the customs, after entry made of any goods, wares or merchandize, on suspicion of fraud, to open and examine, in the presence of two or more reputable merchants, any package or packages thereof, and if upon such examination they shall be found to agree with the entries, the officer making such seizure, shall cause the same to be repacked, and delivered to the owner or claimant forthwith, and the expence of such examination shall be paid by the collector, and allowed in the settlement of his accounts; but if any of the packages so examined be found to differ in their contents from the entry, and it shall appear that such difference hath been made with intention to defraud the revenue, then all the goods, wares or merchandize contained in such package or packages, shall be forfeited: *Provided always*, That if the owner or consignee of such goods as shall not be accompanied with the original invoice, should choose to wait the receipt of the invoice, in such case, the collector shall take into his possession, all such goods, wares and merchandize, and store the same, at the expence

and rifque of the owner or confignee, until the invoice fhall arrive, or until they agree to have the fame valued.

Sec. 24. *And be it further enacted,* That every collector, naval-officer and furveyor, or other perfon fpecially appointed by either of them for that purpofe, fhall have full power and authority, to enter any fhip or veffel, in which they fhall have reafon to fufpect any goods, wares or merchandize fubject to duty fhall be concealed; and therein to fearch for, feize, and fecure any fuch goods, wares or merchandize; and if they fhall have caufe to fufpect a concealment thereof, in any particular dwelling-houfe, ftore, building, or other place, they or either of them, fhall, upon application on oath or affirmation to any juftice of the peace, be entitled to a warrant, to enter fuch houfe, ftore, or other place (in the day time only) and there to fearch for fuch goods, and if any fhall be found, to feize and fecure the fame for trial; and all fuch goods, wares and merchandize, on which the duties fhall not have been paid or fecured, fhall be forfeited. *Goods fubject to duty and concealed, how to be fearched for, feized and fecured.*

Sec. 25. *And be it further enacted,* That all goods, wares and merchandize which fhall be feized by virtue of this act, fhall be put into and remain in the cuftody of the collector, until fuch proceedings fhall be had, as by this act are required, to afcertain whether the fame have been forfeited or not, and if it fhall be adjudged that they are not forfeited, they fhall be forthwith reftored to the owner or owners, claimant or claimants thereof. And if any perfon or perfons fhall conceal or buy any goods, wares or merchandize, knowing them to be liable to feizure by this act, fuch perfon or perfons fhall on conviction thereof, forfeit and pay a fum double the value of the goods fo concealed or purchafed. *Collector to take cuftody of goods feized.* *Penalty for concealing or buying goods fubject to duty.*

Sec. 26. *And be it further enacted,* That it fhall be the duty of the feveral officers to be appointed

Officers may make seizure as well without as within their district.

or employed by virtue of this act, to make seizure of, and secure any ship or vessel, goods, wares or merchandize, which shall be liable to seizure by virtue of this act, as well without, as within their respective districts.

Officers sued or molested may plead this act.

Sec. 27. *And be it further enacted,* That if any officer or other person, executing, or aiding and assisting in the seizure of goods, shall be sued or molested for any thing done in virtue of the powers given by this act, or by virtue of a warrant granted by any judge or justice pursuant to law, such officer or other person may plead the general issue, and give this act in evidence; and if in such suit the plaintiff be non-suited, or judgment pass against him, the defendant shall recover double cost; and in all actions, suits or informations to be brought, where any seizure shall be made pursuant to this act, if the property be claimed by any person, in every such case the onus probandi shall be upon such claimant; and if any person shall forcibly resist, prevent, or impede any officer of the customs, or their deputies, or any person assisting them in the execution of their duty, such persons so offending shall for every offence be fined in a sum not exceeding four hundred dollars.

Collectors, naval officers, and surveyors to enter into bond for performance of duty.

Sec. 28. *And be it further enacted,* That every collector, naval-officer and surveyor, shall within three months after he enters upon the execution of his office, give bond with one or more sufficient sureties, to be approved of by the comptroller of the treasury of the United States, and payable to the said United States, conditioned for the true and faithful discharge of the duties of his office according to law; that is to say, the collector of Philadelphia in the sum of sixty thousand dollars, the collector of New-York, fifty thousand dollars, the collector of Boston, forty thousand dollars, the collectors of Baltimore-town and Charleston, thirty thousand dollars, the collector of Norfolk and

Portſmouth, fifteen thouſand dollars, the collec- Collectors, &c. to enter into bond for performance of duty. tors of Portſmouth in New-Hampſhire, of Salem and Beverly, Wilmington, Annapolis, George-town in Maryland, Bermuda-Hundred and City-point, and Alexandria, ten thouſand dollars each, the collectors of Newburyport, Glouceſter, Marblehead, Plymouth, Nantucket, Portland and Falmouth, New-London, New-Haven, Fairfield, Perth-Amboy, Cheſter, Oxford, York-town, Dumfries, George-town in South-Carolina, Beaufort, and Savannah, each five thouſand dollars, and all the other collectors, in the ſum of two thouſand dollars each. The naval-officers for the ports of Boſton, New-York, Philadelphia, Baltimore-town and Charleſton ten thouſand dollars each, and all the other naval-officers, in the ſum of two thouſand dollars each. The ſurveyors of the ports of Boſton, New-York, Philadelphia, Baltimore-town, and Charleſton, five thouſand dollars each, and all other ſurveyors, one thouſand dollars each, which bonds ſhall be filed in the office of the ſaid comptroller, and be by him ſeverally put in ſuit for the benefit of the United States, upon any breach of the condition thereof.

Sec. 29. *And be it further enacted,* That there Their fees of office and per centage. ſhall be allowed and paid to the collectors, naval-officers and ſurveyors, to be appointed purſuant to this act, the fees and per centage following, that is to ſay; to each collector, for every entrance of any ſhip or veſſel of one hundred tons burthen or upwards, two dollars and an half; for every clearance of any ſhip or veſſel of one hundred tons burthen and upwards, two dollars and an half; for every entrance of any ſhip or veſſel under the burthen of one hundred tons, one dollar and an half; for every clearance of a ſhip or veſſel under one hundred tons burthen, one dollar and an half; for every permit to land goods, twenty cents; for every bond taken officially, forty cents; and for every

Fees of collectors, naval officers and surveyors.

permit to load goods for exportation, which are entitled to a drawback, thirty cents; for every official certificate, twenty cents; for every bill of health, twenty cents; for every other official document (registers excepted) required by the owner or master of every vessel, not before enumerated, twenty cents; and where a naval-officer is appointed to the same port, the said fees shall be equally divided between the collector and the said naval-officer, apportioning to each his moiety of the necessary expences of stationary, and the rent of an office to be provided by the collector, in the place of his residence, most convenient for the trade of the district, in which the said collector and naval-officer shall each have at least one separate room: and the said fees shall be received by the collector, who shall settle the accounts monthly, and pay to the naval-officer the balance which may be due to him on such monthly settlement. To each surveyor there shall be allowed, for all the services required by law, to be performed by such surveyor, on board any ship or vessel of one hundred tons and upwards, and having on board goods, wares and merchandize, subject to duty, three dollars; for the like services on board any ship or vessel of less than one hundred tons burthen, having on board goods, wares and merchandize, subject to duty, one and an half dollars; on all vessels not having on board goods, wares and merchandize subject to duty, two thirds of a dollar; all which fees shall be paid to the collector, by the master or owner of the ship or vessel in which the services are performed, and the said collector shall pay weekly to the surveyor the fees so received; to each inspector there shall be allowed for every day he shall be actually employed in aid of the customs, a sum not exceeding one dollar and twenty-five cents, to be paid by the collector out of the revenue, and charged to the public; to the measurers, weighers and gaugers respectively for their services, shall be allowed, and paid by the collector out of the revenue, for the measurement of every one hundred bushels of salt or grain, eighteen cents ; for the measurement of every one hundred bushels of coal, twenty-five cents ; for the weighing of every one hundred and twelve pounds, one cent ; for the gauging of every cask, six cents. There shall moreover be allowed to the collectors at each of the following ports, to wit : Boston, Salem and Beverly, New-York, Philadelphia, Baltimore, Norfolk or Portsmouth, and Charleston, one half per centum on the amount of all monies by them respectively received and paid into the treasury of the United States ; and to the collector at each of the other ports by this act established, one per centum on the amount of all monies by them respectively received and paid into the treasury of the United States. Every collector, naval-officer and surveyor, shall cause to be affixed, and constantly kept in some public and conspicuous place of his office, a fair table of the rates of fees, and duties demandable by law ; and in case of failure herein, shall forfeit and pay one hundred dollars, to be recovered with costs, in any court having cognizance thereof, to the use of the informer ; and if any officer of the customs shall demand, or receive any greater or other fee, compensation or reward, for executing any duty or service required of him by law, he shall forfeit and pay two hundred dollars for each offence, recoverable in manner aforesaid, for the use of the party grieved.

Fees of collectors, &c.

To set up table of fees.

Penalty for demanding greater or other fees.

Sec. 30. *And be it further enacted,* That the duties and fees to be collected by virtue of this act, shall be received in gold and silver coin only, at the following rates, that is to say, the gold coins of France, England, Spain, and Portugal, and all other gold coin of equal fineness, at eighty-nine

Rates of coins for receiving duties and fees.

_{Rates of coin.} cents for every penny-weight. The Mexican dollar at one hundred cents ; the crown of France at one dollar and eleven cents ; the crown of England at one dollar and eleven cents, and all silver coins of equal fineneſs, at one dollar and eleven cents per ounce.

_{Drawbacks where payable,} Sec. 31. *And be it further enacted*, That all the drawbacks allowed by law on the exportation of goods, wares and merchandize imported, ſhall be paid or allowed by the collector at whoſe office the ſaid goods, wares and merchandize were originally entered, and not otherwiſe, retaining one per centum for the benefit of the United States.

_{and how to be allowed.} Sec. 32. *Provided always, and be it further enacted,* That no goods, wares or merchandize entitled to drawback, ſhall be reladen before an entry ſhall be made with the collector of the port from whence ſuch goods are intended to be exported ; which entry ſhall contain a particular account of the caſks and packages, their marks, numbers and contents, the coſt thereof, the veſſel or veſſels in which they were imported, and the place or places imported from ; and the perſon or perſons intending to export ſuch goods, ſhall give bond, with one or more ſufficient ſureties, that the ſame or any part thereof, ſhall not be relanded in any port or place within the limits of the United States, as ſettled by the late treaty of peace : and ſhall moreover make oath or affirmation as to the truth of the entry, that the goods, wares and merchandize, are in quantity, quality and value, as therein expreſſed, according to the inward entry thereof, which entry was duly made at the time of importation purſuant to the directions of this act ; and that the quality is the ſame as at the time of importation ; and the exporter of ſuch goods ſhall not be entitled to draw back the duties, until at leaſt ſix months after the ex-

portation thereof, and until he shall produce to the collector with whom such outward entry is made, a certificate in writing of two reputable merchants, at the foreign port or place in which the same were landed, together with the oath or affirmation of the master and mate of the vessel in which they were exported, certifying the delivery thereof; but in case any vessel shall be cast away, or meet with such unavoidable accidents as to prevent the landing such goods, a protest in due form of law, made by the master and mate, or some of the seamen, or in case no such protest can be had, then the oath or affirmation of the exporter shall be received in lieu of the other proofs herein directed, unless there shall be good reason to suspect the truth of such oath or affirmation, in which case it shall and may be lawful for the collector to require such further proof as the nature of the case may demand. *Provided also,* That no goods, wares or merchandize imported, shall be entitled to a drawback of the duties paid, or secured to be paid thereon, unless such duties shall amount to twenty dollars at the least; nor unless they shall be exported in the same cask, package or packages, and from the port or district into which they were originally imported, and moreover shall be reladen under the inspection of the collector, naval-officer or surveyor of the port. *Drawbacks, how to be allowed.*

Sec. 33. *And be it further enacted,* That the sums allowed to be paid by law on the exportation of dried or pickled fish, and of salted provisions, shall be paid by the collector of the port or district from whence the same shall be exported: *Provided,* That due entry thereof shall be first made, and bonds given, as in case of drawbacks, and that no such allowance shall be made, unless it shall amount to three dollars at the least upon any one entry. *Allowance on the exportation of dried or pickled fish, and salted provisions, how to be made.*

K

Sec. 34. *And be it further enacted,* That if any goods, wares or merchandize, entered for exportation with a view to draw back the duties, or to obtain any allowance given by law on the exportation thereof, shall be landed in any port or place within the limits of the United States as aforesaid, all such goods, wares and merchandize shall be subject to seizure and forfeiture, together with the vessel from which such goods shall be landed, and the vessels or boats used in landing the same, and all persons concerned therein, shall on indictment and conviction thereof, suffer imprisonment for a term not exceeding six months: and for discovery of frauds, and seizure of goods, wares and merchandize, relanded contrary to law, the several officers established by this act shall have the same powers, and in case of seizure the same proceedings shall be had, as in the case of goods, wares and merchandize imported contrary to law: And for measuring, weighing or gauging goods for exportation, the same fees shall be allowed as in like cases upon the importation thereof.

<small>Goods entitled to drawback or allowance, to be forfeited if landed after entry made.</small>

Sec. 35. *And be it further enacted,* That if any officer of the customs, shall directly or indirectly, take or receive any bribe, reward or recompence for conniving, or shall connive at a false entry of any ship or vessel, or of any goods, wares or merchandize, and shall be thereof convicted, every such officer shall forfeit and pay a sum not less than two hundred, nor more than two thousand dollars for each offence, and be forever disabled from holding any office of trust or profit under the United States; and any person giving or offering any bribe, recompence or reward, for any such deception, collusion or fraud, shall forfeit and pay a sum not less than two hundred, nor more than two thousand dollars for each offence: And in all cases where an oath or affirmation is by this act required from a master or other person,

<small>Penalty on officer receiving a bribe, or conniving at a false entry.</small>

having command of a ship or vessel, or from an owner or consignee of goods, wares and merchandize, if the person so swearing or affirming, shall swear or affirm falsely, such person shall, on indictment and conviction thereof, be punished by fine or imprisonment, or both, in the discretion of the court before whom the conviction shall be had, so as the fine shall not exceed one thousand dollars, and the term of imprisonment, shall not exceed twelve months.

<small>On masters of vessels or others who shall take a false oath.</small>

Sec. 36. *And be it further enacted,* That all penalties accruing by any breach of this act, shall be sued for and recovered with costs of suit, in the name of the United States, in any court proper to try the same, by the collector of the district where the same accrued, and not otherwise, unless in cases of penalty relating to an officer of the customs; and such collector shall be, and hereby is authorised and directed to sue for and prosecute the same to effect, and to distribute and pay the sum recovered, after first deducting all necessary costs and charges, according to law. And all ships or vessels, goods, wares and merchandize, which shall become forfeit by virtue of this act, shall be seized, libelled and prosecuted as aforesaid, in the proper court having cognizance thereof; and the court shall cause fourteen days notice to be given of such seizure and libel, by causing the substance of such libel, with the order of the court thereon, setting forth the time and place appointed for trial, to be inserted in some public newspaper, nearest the place of seizure, and also by posting up the same in the most public manner for the space of fourteen days, at or near the place of trial; and proclamation shall be made in such manner as the court shall direct; and if no person shall appear to claim such ship or vessel, goods, wares or merchandize, the same shall be adjudged to be forfeited; but if any person shall appear before such judg-

<small>Mode of prosecuting and recovering penalties and forfeitures.</small>

Mode of prosecuting and recovering penalties and forfeitures.

ment of forfeiture, and claim any such ship or vessel, goods, wares or merchandize, and shall give bond to defend the prosecution thereof, and to respond the cost in case he shall not support his claim, the court shall proceed to hear and determine the cause according to law: And upon the prayer of any claimant to the court, that any ship or vessel, goods, wares or merchandizes so seized and prosecuted, or any part thereof should be delivered to such claimant, it shall be lawful for the court to appoint three proper persons to appraise such ship or vessel, goods, wares or merchandize, who shall be sworn in open court for the faithful discharge of their duty; and such appraisement shall be made at the expence of the party on whose prayer it is granted; and on the return of such appraisement, if the claimant shall, with one or more sureties, to be approved of by the court, execute a bond in the usual form, to the United States, for the payment of a sum equal to the sum at which the ship or vessel, goods, wares or merchandize so prayed to be delivered, be appraised, the court shall by rule order such ship or vessel, goods, wares or merchandize, to be delivered to the said claimant, and the said bond shall be lodged with the proper officer of the court; and if judgment shall pass in favour of the claimant, the court shall cause the said bond to be cancelled; but if judgment shall pass against the claimant, as to the whole or any part of such ship or vessel, goods, wares or merchandize, and the claimant shall not within twenty days thereafter pay into the court the amount of the appraised value of such ship or vessel, goods, wares or merchandize so condemned, with the costs, the bond shall be put in suit. And when any prosecution shall be commenced on account of the seizure of any ship or vessel, goods, wares or merchandize, and judgment shall be given for the claimant or claimants; if it shall appear to the court before whom such prosecution shall be tried, that there was a reasonable cause of seizure, the same court shall cause a proper certificate or entry to be made thereof, and in such case the claimant shall not be entitled to costs, nor shall the person who made the seizure, or the prosecutor be liable to action, judgment or suit, on account of such seizure or prosecution. *Provided*, That the ship or vessel, goods, wares or merchandize be after judgment forthwith returned to such claimant or claimants, his or their agents : *And provided*, That no action or prosecution shall be maintained in any case under this act, unless the same shall have been commenced within three years next after the penalty or forfeiture was incurred.

_{Mode of prosecuting and recovering penalties and forfeitures.}

Sec. 37. *And be it further enacted*, That all ships, vessels, goods, wares or merchandize, which shall be condemned by virtue of this act, shall be sold by the proper officer of the court in which such condemnation shall be had, to the highest bidder at public auction, by order of such court, and at such place as the court may appoint, giving at least fifteen days notice (except in case of perishable goods) in one or more of the public newspapers of the place where such sale shall be, or if no paper is published in such place, in one or more of the papers published in the nearest place thereto.

_{Vessels or goods condemned by virtue of this act, how to be sold, and by whom.}

Sec. 38. *And be it further enacted*, That all penalties, fines and forfeitures, recovered by virtue of this act (and not otherwise appropriated) shall, after deducting all proper costs and charges, be disposed of as follows : One moiety shall be for the use of the United States, and paid into the treasury thereof; the other moiety shall be divided into three equal parts, and paid to the collector, naval-officer and surveyor of the district wherein the same shall have been incurred ; and in such districts where only two of the aforesaid officers shall

_{Appropriation of fines, penalties & forfeitures.}

[74]

<small>Appropriation of fines, penalties & forfeitures.</small> have been established, the said moiety shall be equally divided between them; and in such districts where only one of the aforesaid officers shall have been established, the said moiety shall be given to such officer: *Provided nevertheless*, That in all cases where such penalties, fines and forfeitures, shall be recovered in pursuance of information given to such collector, by any person, other than the said naval-officer and surveyor, the one half of such moiety shall be given to the informer, and the remainder thereof shall be disposed of between the collector, naval-officer and surveyor, in manner and form as above limited and expressed.

<small>R. Island & N. Carolina.</small> *And whereas*, The states of Rhode-Island and Providence Plantations, and North-Carolina, have not as yet ratified the present Constitution of the United States, by reason whereof this act doth not extend to the collecting of duties within either of the said two states, and it is thereby become necessary that the following provision with respect to goods, wares or merchandize imported from either of the said two states should for the present year take place:

<small>Goods imported from, subject to same duties as from foreign countries.</small> Sec. 39. *Be it therefore further enacted*, That all goods, wares and merchandize not of their own growth or manufacture, which shall be imported from either of the said two states of Rhode-Island and Providence Plantations, or North-Carolina, into any other port or place within the limits of the United States, as settled by the late treaty of peace, shall be subject to the like duties, seizures and forfeitures, as goods wares or merchandize imported from any state or country without the said limits.

<small>Dutiable goods of foreign growth</small> Sec. 40. *And be it further enacted*, That no goods, wares or merchandize of foreign growth or manufacture, subject to the payment of duties, shall be brought into the United States, in any other manner than by sea, nor in any ship or ves-

sel less than thirty tons burthen, except within ^{brought in-} the district of Louisville, and except also in such ^{to the U.} ^{States ex-} vessels as are now actually on their voyages ; nor ^{cept by sea,} shall be landed, or unladen, at any other place ^{& in certain} ^{vessels sub-} than is by this act directed, under the penalty of ^{ject to for-} seizure and forfeiture, of all such vessels, goods, ^{feiture.} wares or merchandize, brought in, landed, or unladen in any other manner. And all goods, wares and merchandize brought into the United States by land, contrary to this act, shall be forfeited, together with the carriages, horses, and oxen, that shall be employed in conveying the same.

FREDERICK AUGUSTUS MUHLENBERG,
Speaker of the House of Representatives.

JOHN ADAMS, *Vice-President of the United States,*
and President of the Senate.

APPROVED, July the 31st, 1789.

GEORGE WASHINGTON,
President of the United States.

CHAPTER VI.

An ACT *for settling the* ACCOUNTS *between the United States and individual States.*

Section 1. **B**E *it enacted by the* SENATE *and* HOUSE *of* REPRESENTATIVES *of the United States of America in Congress assembled,* That the President of the United States be, and he ^{Vacancies} hereby is empowered to nominate, and by and with ^{in the board} the advice and consent of the Senate, to appoint ^{of commis-} ^{sioners, how} such person or persons as he may think proper for ^{to be suppli-} supplying any vacancy that now is, or may here- ^{ed.} after take place in the Board of Commissioners, established by an ordinance of the late Congress, of the seventh of May, one thousand seven hundred and eighty-seven, to carry into effect the said ordinance and resolutions of Congress, for the settlement of accounts between the United States and individual states.

Clerks to be appointed,

Sec. 2. *And be it further enacted,* That the said Board of Commissioners be, and they hereby are empowered to appoint a chief clerk, and such other clerks as the duties of their office may require;

their salaries.

and that the pay of the said chief clerk be six hundred dollars per annum, and of each other clerk four hundred dollars per annum.

FREDERICK AUGUSTUS MUHLENBERG,
Speaker of the House of Representatives.

JOHN ADAMS, *Vice-President of the United States, and President of the Senate.*

APPROVED, August the 5th, 1789.
GEORGE WASHINGTON,
President of the United States.

CHAPTER VII.

An ACT *to establish an Executive Department, to be denominated the* DEPARTMENT *of* WAR.

Section 1. BE *it enacted by the* SENATE *and* HOUSE *of* REPRESENTATIVES *of the United States of America in Congress assembled,*

Sec'ry for the department of war, his duty.

That there shall be an executive department, to be denominated the Department of War; and that there shall be a principal officer therein, to be called the Secretary for the Department of War, who shall perform and execute such duties as shall from time to time be enjoined on, or entrusted to him by the President of the United States, agreeably to the Constitution, relative to military commissions, or to the land or naval forces, ships, or warlike stores of the United States, or to such other matters respecting military or naval affairs, as the President of the United States shall assign to the said department, or relative to the granting of lands to persons entitled thereto, for military services rendered to the United States, or relative to Indian affairs: And furthermore, that the said principal officer shall conduct the business of the said department in such manner, as the President of the United States shall from time to time order or instruct.

Sec. 2. *And be it further enacted*, That there shall be in the said department, an inferior officer, to be appointed by the said principal officer, to be employed therein as he shall deem proper, and to be called the chief clerk in the department of war, and who, whenever the said principal officer shall be removed from office by the President of the United States, or in any other case of vacancy, shall during such vacancy, have the charge and custody of all records, books and papers, appertaining to the said department. Principal clerk, his duty.

Sec. 3. *And be it further enacted*, That the said principal officer, and every other person to be appointed or employed in the said department, shall, before he enters on the execution of his office or employment, take an oath or affirmation well and faithfully to execute the trust committed to him. Oath of office.

Sec. 4. *And be it further enacted*, That the Secretary for the department of war, to be appointed in consequence of this act, shall forthwith after his appointment, be entitled to have the custody and charge of all records, books and papers in the office of Secretary for the department of war, heretofore established by the United States in Congress assembled. Secretary to take charge of papers, &c. of war department.

FREDERICK AUGUSTUS MUHLENBERG,
Speaker of the House of Representatives.

JOHN ADAMS, *Vice-President of the United States, and President of the Senate.*

APPROVED, August 7th, 1789.

GEORGE WASHINGTON,
President of the United States.

CHAPTER VIII.

An ACT *to provide for the* GOVERNMENT *of the Territory North-West of the River* OHIO.

Recital.

WHEREAS in order that the ordinance of the United States in Congress assembled, for the government of the territory north-west of the river Ohio may continue to have full effect, it is requisite that certain provisions should be made, so as to adapt the same to the present Constitution of the United States:

Governor to make communication to the President of the U. States.

Section 1. *Be it enacted by the* SENATE *and* HOUSE *of* REPRESENTATIVES *of the United States of America in Congress assembled,* That in all cases in which by the said ordinance, any information is to be given, or communication made by the Governor of the said territory to the United States in Congress assembled, or to any of their officers, it shall be the duty of the said Governor to give such information and to make such communication to the President of the United States; and the President shall

Officers, how to be appointed,

nominate, and by and with the advice and consent of the Senate, shall appoint all officers which by the said ordinance were to have been appointed by the United States in Congress assembled, and all

Commissioned & removed.

officers so appointed, shall be commissioned by him; and in all cases where the United States in Congress assembled, might, by the said ordinance, revoke any commission or remove from any office, the President is hereby declared to have the same powers of revocation and removal.

In cases of death, removal, &c. secretary to execute the power of governor during such vacancy.

Sec. 2. *And be it further enacted,* That in case of the death, removal, resignation, or necessary absence of the Governor of the said territory, the Secretary thereof shall be, and he is hereby authorised and required to execute all the powers, and perform all the duties of the Governor, during the vacancy occasioned by the removal, resignation or necessary absence of the said Governor.

FREDERICK AUGUSTUS MUHLENBERG,
Speaker of the House of Representatives.

JOHN ADAMS, *Vice-President of the United States, and President of the Senate.*

APPROVED, August the 7th, 1789.

GEORGE WASHINGTON,
President of the United States.

CHAPTER IX.

An ACT *for the establishment and support of* LIGHT-HOUSES, BEACONS, BUOYS, *and* PUBLIC PIERS.

Section 1. BE *it enacted by the* SENATE *and* HOUSE *of* REPRESENTATIVES *of the United States of America in Congress assembled,* That all expences which shall accrue from and after the fifteenth day of August, one thousand seven hundred and eighty-nine, in the necessary support, maintenance and repairs of all light-houses, beacons, buoys and public piers erected, placed, or sunk before the passing of this act, at the entrance of, or within any bay, inlet, harbour, or port of the United States, for rendering the navigation thereof easy and safe, shall be defrayed out of the treasury of the United States : *Provided nevertheless,* That none of the said expences shall continue to be so defrayed by the United States, after the expiration of one year from the day aforesaid, unless such light-houses, beacons, buoys and public piers, shall in the mean time be ceded to, and vested in the United States, by the state or states respectively in which the same may be, together with the lands and tenements thereunto belonging, and together with the jurisdiction of the same.

[margin: Expences after 15th Aug. 1789, to be defrayed out of treasury of U. States. *]*

[margin: Provided a cession be made within one year. *]*

Light house to be erected near entrance of Chesapeake Bay.

Sec. 2. *And be it further enacted,* That a light-house shall be erected near the entrance of Chesapeake-Bay, at such place, when ceded to the United States in manner aforesaid, as the President of the United States shall direct.

Secretary of treasury to contract for building, repairing, &c. when necessary.

Sec. 3. *And be it further enacted,* That it shall be the duty of the Secretary of the Treasury to provide by contracts, which shall be approved by the President of the United States, for building a light-house near the entrance of Chesapeake-Bay, and for rebuilding when necessary, and keeping in good repair, the light-houses, beacons, buoys, and public piers in the several states, and for furnishing the same with all necessary supplies; and also to agree for the salaries, wages, or hire of the person or persons appointed by the President, for the superintendance and care of the same.

Pilots to be regulated by the existing laws of the respective states.

Sec. 4. *And be it further enacted,* That all pilots in the bays, inlets, rivers, harbours and ports of the United States, shall continue to be regulated in conformity with the existing laws of the states respectively wherein such pilots may be, or with such laws as the states may respectively hereafter enact for the purpose, until further legislative provision shall be made by Congress.

FREDERICK AUGUSTUS MUHLENBERG,
Speaker of the House of Representatives.

JOHN ADAMS, *Vice-President of the United States, and President of the Senate.*

Approved, August the 7th, 1789.

GEORGE WASHINGTON,
President of the United States.

CHAPTER X.

An ACT *providing for the* EXPENCES *which may attend* NEGOCIATIONS *or* TREATIES *with the* INDIAN TRIBES, *and the appointment of* COMMISSIONERS *for managing the same.*

Section 1. BE it enacted by the SENATE and HOUSE of REPRESENTATIVES *of the United States of America in Congress assembled,* That a sum not exceeding twenty thousand dollars, arising from the duties on imports and tonnage, shall be, and the same is hereby appropriated to defraying the expence of negociating and treating with the Indian tribes.

<small>Sum appropriated.</small>

Sec. 2. *And be it further enacted,* That each of the commissioners who may be appointed for managing such negociations and treaties, shall be entitled to an allowance, exclusive of his expences at the place of treaty, of eight dollars per day during his actual service, to be paid out of the monies so appropriated.

<small>Allowance to commissioners.</small>

FREDERICK AUGUSTUS MUHLENBERG,
Speaker of the House of Representatives.

JOHN ADAMS, *Vice-President of the United States, and President of the Senate.*

APPROVED, August the 20th, 1789.

GEORGE WASHINGTON,
President of the United States.

CHAPTER XI.

An ACT *for* REGISTERING *and* CLEARING VESSELS, REGULATING *the* COASTING TRADE, *and for other Purposes.*

Section 1. BE it enacted by the SENATE and HOUSE *of* REPRESENTATIVES *of the United States of America in Congress assembled,* That any ship or vessel built within the United

[82]

<small>What ships or vessels may be registered.</small> States, and belonging wholly to a citizen or citizens thereof, or not built within the said States, but on the sixteenth day of May, one thousand seven hundred and eighty-nine, belonging, and thereafter continuing to belong wholly to a citizen or citizens thereof, and of which the master is a citizen of the United States, and no other, may be registered in manner herein after provided, and being so registered, shall be deemed and taken to be, and denominated, a ship or vessel of the United States, and entitled to the benefits granted by any law of the United States, to ships or vessels of the descriptions aforesaid.

<small>Persons registering to obtain a certificate.</small> Sec. 2. *And be it further enacted*, That the person or persons claiming property in any such ship or vessel, in order to entitle her to the benefits aforesaid, shall cause the same to be registered, and shall obtain a certificate of such registry from the collector of the district to which such ship or vessel belongs, in manner hereinafter directed, which certificate, attested by the Secretary of the Treasury, under his hand and seal, and countersigned by the collector, shall be in the form following, viz.

<small>Form of the certificate.</small> " IN pursuance of an act of the Congress of the United States of America, entitled, " An act for registering and clearing vessels, regulating the coasting trade, and for other purposes," [here insert the name, occupation and residence of the subscribing owner] having taken and subscribed the oath or affirmation required by the said act, and having sworn or affirmed, that he, together with [names, occupation, and residence of non-subscribing owners] is (or are) sole owner (or owners) of the ship (or vessel) called the [ship's name] of [place to which the ship or vessel belongs] whereof [master's name] is at present master, and is a citizen of the United States, and that the said ship (or vessel) was [when and where built] and [name of surveying

officer] having certified to us, that the said ship or vessel, has [number of decks] and masts, that her length is   her breadth   her depth   and that she measures   tons, that she is [here describe the vessel and how built] has   gallery and   head : And the said subscribing owners having consented and agreed to the above description and measurement, and having caused sufficient security to be given as is required by the said act, the said [kind of vessel and name] has been duly registered at the port of   Given under our hands and seals of office, at [port] this   day of   in the year [words at full length.] And the collector shall transmit to the Secretary of the Treasury a duplicate of every such certificate so granted. And it shall be the duty of the Secretary of the Treasury to transmit to the collectors of the several ports of the United States, a sufficient number of certificates attested under his hand and seal, leaving the blanks to be filled up by the collectors respectively.

Form of the certificate.

Sec. 3. *And be it further enacted,* That to ascertain the tonnage of all ships or vessels, the surveyor or other person appointed by the collector to measure the same, shall take the length of every vessel, if double decked, from the fore part of the main stem to the after part of the stern post above the upper deck, the breadth at the broadest part above the main wales, and half such breadth shall be accounted the depth of every double decked vessel ; he shall then deduct from the length three fifths of the breadth, multiply the remainder by the breadth, and the product by the depth, dividing the product of the whole by ninety-five, the quotient shall be deemed the true contents or tonnage of such ship or vessel. To ascertain the tonnage of every single decked vessel, he shall take the length

Rule for ascertaining the tonnage of ships or vessels.

and breadth, as is directed to be taken for double decked vessels, and deduct three fifths in like manner, and the depth from the under side of the deck plank to the cieling in the hold, and shall multiply and divide as aforesaid, and the quotient shall be deemed the true contents or tonnage of such single decked vessel.

<small>The port to which registered ships or vessels belong ascertained; & the name painted on stern.</small>

Sec. 4. *And be it further enacted,* That the port to which any such ship or vessel shall be deemed to belong, agreeably to the intent and meaning of this act, shall be the port at or near which the husband or acting and managing owner or owners of such ship or vessel usually resides or reside: And the name of such ship or vessel, and of the place to which she belongs shall be painted on her stern, on a black ground with white letters of not less than three inches in length.

<small>Vessels of citizens residing in foreign countries not entitled to register but in certain cases</small>

Sec. 5. *And be it further enacted,* That no ship or vessel owned in whole or in part by any citizen of the United States, usually residing in any foreign country, shall, during the time he shall continue so to reside, be deemed a vessel of the United States, entitled to be registered by virtue of this act, unless he be an agent for, and partner in, some house or co-partnership, consisting of citizens of the United States, actually carrying on trade in the said States.

<small>No registry to be made or certificate granted until an oath be taken.</small>

Sec. 6. *And be it further enacted,* That no registry shall be made or certificate granted, until the following oath or affirmation be taken and subscribed, before the officer herein before authorised to make such registry and grant such certificate, (which oath or affirmation such officer is hereby empowered to administer) by the owner of such ship or vessel, if owned by one person only, or in case there shall be two or more owners, then by any one of such owners; namely,

" I, of [place

of residence and occupation] do swear or affirm, that the ship or vessel   of   [take the description from the certificate of the surveyor or other person authorised by this act] was built at   in the year   or was the entire property of   on the sixteenth day of May, one thousand seven hundred and eighty-nine, and hath continued to be the property of a citizen or citizens of the United States, that   the present master, is a citizen of the United States, and that I,   and [the other owners names, occupation, and where they respectively reside, viz. town, place, county and state, or if resident in a foreign country, being an agent for, or partner in any house or co-partnership] am or are sole owner or owners of the said ship or vessel, and that no other person whatever hath any property therein, and that I, the said   [and the said owners, if any] am or are truly a citizen or citizens of the United States, and that no foreigner, directly or indirectly, hath any part or interest in the said ship or vessel."

Form of the oath.

 Sec. 7. *Provided always, and be it further enacted,* That whenever the owner or owners of such ship or vessel, usually resides or reside out of the district within which such ship or vessel may be at the time of granting the certificate of registry, that such owner, or where there are two or more owners, any one of them may take and subscribe the said oath or affirmation, before the collector of the district within which he usually resides, omitting in the said oath or affirmation the description of such ship or vessel, as expressed in the certificate of the surveyor, and inserting in lieu thereof, the name of the port and district within which such ship or vessel may then be; and the collector before whom such oath or affirmation may be taken and subscrib-

Certificates of registry may be granted in one district, the owners residing in another.

ed, shall transmit the same to the collector of the district where such ship or vessel may be, upon the receipt whereof the said collector shall proceed to register such ship or vessel, in like manner as though the usual and regular oath or affirmation had been taken and subscribed before him.

<small>Surveyor to measure vessels in presence of master, or other person, on the part of the owners.</small>

Sec. 8. *And be it further enacted,* That the surveyor or other person, to be appointed in pursuance of this act, shall, previous to the registering or granting of any certificate of registry, as aforesaid, examine and measure such ship or vessel, as to all and every particular contained in the form of the certificate aforesaid, in the presence of the master, or of any other person to be appointed for that purpose on the part of the owner or owners, and shall deliver a just and true account in writing of the built, description, and measurement of every such ship or vessel as are specified in the form of the certificate above recited, to the person authorised as aforesaid, to make such registry and grant such certificate thereof; and the said master or other person attending on the part of the owner or owners, is hereby required to sign his name also to the certificate of the surveying or examining officer, or other person duly appointed, in testimony of the truth thereof, provided such master or other person, shall agree to the several particulars therein set forth and described.

<small>Master, &c. to give bond not to dispose of certificate of registry.</small>

Sec. 9. *And be it further enacted,* That when the certificate of registry aforesaid shall be granted, sufficient security by bond, shall be given to the collector in behalf of the United States, by the master and owner or owners, or by some other person or persons on his, her, or their behalf, such security to be approved of by the collector, in the penalties following, that is to say; if such ship or vessel shall be above the burthen of fifteen, and not exceeding fifty tons, in the penalty of four

hundred dollars, if exceeding the burthen of fifty tons, and not exceeding one hundred tons, in the penalty of eight hundred dollars, if exceeding the burthen of one hundred tons, and not exceeding two hundred tons, in the penalty of twelve hundred dollars, if exceeding the burthen of two hundred tons, and not exceeding three hundred tons, in the penalty of sixteen hundred dollars; and if exceeding the burthen of three hundred tons, in the penalty of two thousand dollars. And the condition of every such bond shall be, that such certificate shall not be sold, lent, or otherwise disposed of to any person or persons whomsoever, and that the same shall be solely used for the ship or vessel to which it is granted, and that in case such ship or vessel shall be lost or taken by an enemy, burnt, or broken up, or otherwise prevented from returning to the port to which she belongs, the certificate, if preserved, shall be delivered up within three months after the arrival of the master in any port or place in the United States, to the collector of the district where he shall arrive; and that if any foreigner, or any person or persons for his use and benefit, shall purchase or otherwise become entitled to the whole or any part or share of, or interest in such ship or vessel, and the same shall be within any district of the United States, in such case the certificate of registry, shall, within seven days after such purchase or transfer of property in such ship or vessel, be delivered up to the collector of the said district; and in case such ship or vessel shall be in any foreign port or place, or at sea when such transfer of interest or property shall take place, the said master shall, within eight days after his arrival in any port or place within the United States, deliver up the said certificate to the collector of the district where he shall arrive; and all the certificates so delivered up, shall be forthwith transmitted by the collector to the Secretary of the Treasury to be cancelled.

In cases of transfer to foreigners, certificate of registry to be delivered up.

[88]

Vessel to be registered anew.

Sec. 10. *And be it further enacted,* That whenever any ship or vessel registered in conformity with this act, shall in whole or in part be sold or transferred to a citizen or citizens of the United States, the former certificate of registry shall be delivered up to the collector, and by him without delay transmitted to the Secretary of the Treasury to be cancelled, and such ship or vessel shall be registered anew by her former name, and a certificate thereof shall be granted by the collector, in like manner as is herein before directed.

A recital of certificate to be made in instruments of transfer.

Sec. 11. *And be it further enacted,* That whenever any such ship or vessel shall in whole or in part be sold or transferred to any person or persons, the certificate of the registry of every such ship or vessel, shall be recited at length in the instrument of transfer or sale thereof, and in default thereof, such instrument of sale or transfer shall be void, and such ship or vessel shall not be deemed or denominated a ship or vessel entitled to any of the benefits or advantages of a ship or vessel of the United States.

Master of a vessel being changed, collector shall endorse it on certificate.

Sec. 12. *And be it further enacted,* That whenever the master or other person having the charge or command of any ship or vessel registered in manner herein before directed, shall be changed, the master or owner of such ship or vessel shall deliver to the collector of the district where such change shall take place, the certificate of registry of such ship or vessel, who shall thereon endorse and subscribe a memorandum of such change, and forthwith give notice of the same to the collector of the district where such ship or vessel was last registered pursuant to this act, who shall likewise make a memorandum of the same in the book of registers, and transmit a copy thereof to the Secretary of the Treasury.

Sec. 13. *And be it further enacted,* That if the certificate of regiftry of any fhip or veffel fhall be loft or deftroyed, the mafter or other perfon having charge of the faid fhip or veffel, may make oath or affirmation before the collector of the diftrict where fuch fhip or veffel may arrive, who is hereby authorifed to adminifter the fame in the words and form following:

In cafes of lofs of certificate, the mafter to make oath.

" I,   being mafter, or having charge of the fhip or veffel called the   do fwear, or affirm, that the faid fhip or veffel hath been, as I verily believe, regiftered according to law by the name of   and that a certificate thereof was granted at the port of   but that the fame is loft or deftroyed (as the cafe may be) and that the fame, if found again, and comes again within my power, fhall be delivered up to the collector of the port where it was granted; and that the mafter of faid fhip or veffel is a citizen of the United States; and that the faid fhip or veffel is, as I believe, the entire property of a citizen or citizens of the United States; and that no foreigner has, to my knowledge and belief, any property or intereft therein:" and the faid oath or affirmation fhall be filed in the office of the faid collector before whom it was made, who is hereby required to regifter the faid veffel anew by her former name, and take the fecurity in manner herein before directed, and deliver the certificate of fuch regiftry to the owner or owners, if refiding within his diftrict, or if not refident there, to the mafter or other perfon having charge of faid fhip or veffel, that fuch certificate of regiftry is granted in purfuance of this act, inftead of a former certificate of regiftry, which appears by fuch proof as this act requires, to be loft; and fuch certificate of regiftry fhall have the fame effect with the original, and the faid collector fhall, within three months, tranfmit a duplicate of the

Form of the oath.

Collector to regifter the veffel anew by her former name,

[90]

said certificate to the Secretary of the Treasury, to be registered in his office, who shall notify the collector who granted the certificate which was lost or destroyed, of the same, who is hereby required to cause a memorandum thereof to be made in his book of registers.

<small>Registered ships or vessels being altered, to be registered anew.</small>

Sec. 14. *And be it further enacted,* That if any ship or vessel, after having been registered in pursuance of this act, shall in any manner whatever, be altered in form or burthen, by being lengthened or built upon, or from one denomination to another, by the mode or method of rigging or fitting, in such case, such vessel shall be registered anew by her former name in manner herein before directed, as soon as she returns to the port to which she belongs, or to any other port in which she may be lawfully registered by virtue of this act, otherwise such ship or vessel shall not be deemed and considered as a ship or vessel of the United States.

<small>Manner of numbering registers.</small>

Sec. 15. *And be it further enacted,* That the collector of every district where registers shall be made and certificates granted in pursuance of this act, shall progressively number the same as they shall be severally granted, beginning at the time when this act shall be in force, and continuing to the end of the present year, and thenceforth beginning at the commencement of every year, and shall enter an exact copy of such certificate with the number thereof, in a book to be kept for that purpose, and shall within three months transmit to the Secretary of the Treasury, a true copy, together with the number of every certificate which shall be by him so granted.

<small>Vessels built in U. States after 15th Aug. 1789,</small>

Sec. 16. *And be it further enacted,* That every ship or vessel built in the United States after the fifteenth day of August, one thousand seven hundred and eighty-nine, and belonging wholly or in

part to the subjects of foreign powers, shall be re- *and owned by foreigners, to be recorded:* corded in the office of the collector of the district in which such ship or vessel was built, in manner following, that is to say: The builder of every *builder to make oath.* such ship or vessel shall make oath or affirmation before the collector of such district, who is hereby authorised to administer such oath in manner following: I,   of [here insert the *Form of the oath.* place of residence, county and state] shipwright, do swear, or affirm, that [here designate the kind of vessel] named   having [number of decks] and being in length   in breadth   in depth   and measuring   tons, having   gallery and   head, was built by me, or under my direction, at [place, county and state] in the United States, in the year   which oath or affirmation shall *The oath to be recorded.* be recorded in manner herein before directed, in a book to be kept for that purpose.

Sec. 17. *And be it further enacted,* That a certificate of the said record, attested under the hand *Collector to grant certificate of record.* and seal of the collector of the district as aforesaid, shall be granted to the master of every such ship or vessel, in manner following: In pursuance of an act, entitled, "An act   I,   collector of the *Form of the certificate.* district of   in the United States, do certify, that the builder [name] of [place of residence, county and state] having sworn or affirmed, that the ship or vessel [here designate the kind of vessel] named   whereof   is at present master, was built at [place, county and state where built] by him or under his direction, in the year   and [here insert the name of the surveyor, or other person appointed by the collector, where there is no surveyor] having certified that the said ship or vessel has [numbers of decks,] is in length ·

[92]

<small>Form of the certificate.</small>

      in breadth   in depth
    and meafures   tons ;
and the faid builder and mafter having agreed to the faid defcription and meafurement, the faid fhip or veffel has been recorded in the diftrict of   in the United States. Witnefs my hand and feal, this day of in the year ," which certificate fhall be recorded in the office of the collector, and a duplicate thereof tranfmitted to the Secretary of the Treafury of the United States, to be recorded in his office.

<small>Surveyor & mafter to give a defcription of veffel to the collector.</small>

  Sec. 18. *And be it further enacted*, That the furveyor or other perfon to be appointed by the collector as aforefaid, is hereby required to deliver a true account in writing, figned with his name, of the built, defcription and meafurement of every fuch fhip or veffel, as fpecified in the form of the faid certificate of record, of fuch fhips or veffels, which account fhall alfo be figned by the mafter, to the collector of the diftrict where fuch certificate of the record fhall be granted.

<small>Veffel's name, or mafter being changed, certificate to be endorfed, otherwife not deemed as recorded.</small>

  Sec. 19. *And be it further enacted*, That if the mafter or the name of any fhip or veffel fo recorded fhall be changed, the owner, part owner or confignee of fuch fhip or veffel fhall caufe a memorandum thereof to be endorfed on the certificate of the record, by the collector of the diftrict where fuch fhip or veffel may be, or at which fhe fhall arrive, if fuch change took place in a foreign country, and a copy thereof fhall be entered in the book of records, a tranfcript whereof fhall be tranfmitted by the collector to the collector of the diftrict where fuch certificate was granted, who fhall enter the fame in his book of records, and forward a duplicate of fuch entry to the Secretary of the Treafury of the United States ; and in fuch cafe, until the faid owner, part owner or confignee fhall

cause the said memorandum to be made by the collector in manner aforesaid, such ship or vessel shall not be deemed or considered as a vessel recorded in pursuance of this act.

Sec. 20. *And be it further enacted,* That the master or other person having command of any ship or vessel recorded in pursuance of this act, shall on entry of such ship or vessel produce the certificate of such record, to the collector of the district, in failure of which the said ship or vessel shall not be entitled to the privileges of a vessel recorded as aforesaid. Master to produce certificate of record to collector.

Sec. 21. *And be it further enacted,* That all the penalties and forfeitures inflicted and incurred by this act, shall, and may be sued for, prosecuted and recovered in such courts, and be disposed of in such manner as any penalties or forfeitures inflicted, or which may be incurred for any offence committed against the United States, in and by an act, entitled, " An act to regulate the collection of the duties imposed by law, on the tonnage of ships or vessels, and on goods, wares and merchandizes, imported into the United States," may legally be sued for, prosecuted, recovered and disposed of. Penalties & forfeitures, how sued for.

Sec. 22. *And be it further enacted,* That from and after the tenth day of September next, every ship or vessel of the burthen of twenty tons or upwards, built within the United States, and wholly owned by a citizen or citizens thereof; or not built within the United States, and on the sixteenth day of May, one thousand seven hundred and eighty-nine, wholly owned and thereafter continuing to be owned by a citizen or citizens of the United States, but not registered, if destined from district to district, or to the bank or whale fisheries, shall, in order to be entitled to all the privileges of a ship or vessel belonging to the United States, employed in the coasting trade or in the fisheries, be enrolled by the Vessels of 20 tons or upwards, employed between district & district, or in the bank or whale fisheries, their privileges.

collector of the district where the owner, or one of the owners of such vessel may reside, and every vessel so enrolled, shall have her name and the name of the place to which she belongs painted on her stern, in manner directed by this act, for registered vessels, and such collector on due proof by oath or affirmation to him made by the owner or one of the owners of such ship or vessel of her name, burthen and denomination, and that she is of the description aforesaid, and of the names of the owner or owners, and of the master thereof, and that they are citizens of the United States, and of the place or places of residence of such owner or owners, shall enroll in a book to be kept for that purpose, the name of every such vessel, her burthen, where built, and denomination, the name or names, and place or places of residence of the owner or owners thereof, and that he or they, together with the master, are citizens of the United States, a description of the built of such vessel as aforesaid, and the date of the enrollment, and shall also grant to the owner or owners, a certificate, containing a copy of such enrollment, and transmit to the Secretary of the Treasury a copy of every such certificate of enrollment, to be by him recorded: And whenever the property of such ship or vessel shall be changed in whole or in part, the person or persons who shall then be owner or owners, or one of them, shall make known such change to the collector of the district where he or they may reside, and such collector is hereby authorised and directed to grant a new certificate of the enrollment of such ship or vessel by her former name, to such owner or owners, upon his or their delivering up the former certificate, which shall be sent to the office of the collector from whence it was issued, to be cancelled: *Provided*, That the master or owner of every vessel of less than twenty tons burthen, and not less than five tons, which

Marginalia:
Name to be painted on the stern.

Collector, upon owners making oath of the name, &c. to enroll the same and grant a certificate.

Vessels between 20 and 5 tons,

shall be employed between any of the districts in the United States, shall cause the name of such vessel and of the place to which she belongs, to be painted on her stern in manner directed by this act for registered vessels, and shall annually procure a licence from the collector of the district to which such vessel belongs, who is hereby authorised to give the same, purporting that such vessel is exempt from clearing and entering for the term of one year from the date thereof; and the master or owner of every such vessel shall give bond with sufficient security for the payment of two hundred dollars to the United States, with condition that such vessel shall not be employed in any illicit trade or commerce; and before any new licence shall be given for a succeeding year to the master of such vessel, he shall on oath or affirmation, declare that no illicit trade has been carried on in such vessel to his knowledge or belief during the time for which she was licensed.

name to be painted on stern, & licence granted by collector for 1 year to exempt them from clearing and entering.

Sec. 23. *And be it further enacted,* That the master, commander or owner of every ship or vessel of the burthen of twenty tons or upwards, to be employed in trade between different districts in the United States, and of every vessel to be employed in the bank or whale fisheries, having a certificate of registry or enrollment, as is herein directed, shall, upon application to the collector of the district where such vessel may lie, be entitled to receive a licence to trade between the different districts in the United States, or to carry on the bank or whale fishery for one year, and it shall be the duty of the collector to grant the same; but no licence shall be granted for any vessel until the owner or owners applying therefor, shall have paid the tonnage duty thereon, and shall enter into bond, with sufficient security, for the payment of one thousand dollars to the United States, with condition, that such vessel shall not within the time

Vessels of 20 tons or upwards registered or enrolled, entitled to a licence for one year.

for which such licence was granted, be employed in any illicit trade or commerce: And if any vessel of the burthen of twenty tons or upwards, not having a certificate of registry or enrollment, and a licence, shall be found trading between different districts, or be employed in the bank or whale fisheries, every such ship or vessel shall be subject to the same tonnage, and fees, as foreign ships or vessels.

<small>Master of vessels outward bound to deliver a manifest & obtain a clearance.</small>

Sec. 24. *And be it further enacted,* That the master or commander of every ship or vessel bound to any foreign port, shall deliver to the collector of the district where such ship or vessel may be, a manifest of the cargo on board such ship or vessel, and on making oath or affirmation to the truth thereof, it shall be the duty of the said collector, to grant a clearance for such ship or vessel, and her loading; and if any ship or vessel bound to any foreign port, shall depart from the place of her loading without such clearance, the master, commander, consignee, or owner thereof, shall forfeit and pay the sum of two hundred dollars for every such offence.

<small>Penalty for failing without.</small>

<small>Master of vessels of 20 tons or upwards trading from district to district & having certain goods, to deliver two manifests.</small>

Sec. 25. *And be it further enacted,* That the master of every ship or vessel of the burthen of twenty tons or upwards, licenced to trade between the different districts of the United States, having on board goods, wares or merchandize of foreign growth or manufacture, of the value of two hundred dollars, or rum or other ardent spirits exceeding four hundred gallons, and being bound from one district to another, shall deliver to the collector, and where the collector and surveyor reside at different places within the same district, to the collector or surveyor, as the one or the other may reside at or nearest to the port where such ship or vessel may be, duplicate manifests of the whole cargo on board such ship or vessel, whether such

cargo shall consist wholly of goods, wares, or merchandize of foreign growth or manufacture, or partly of such goods, wares or merchandize, and partly of goods, wares, or merchandize, the growth or manufacture of the United States, specifying therein the name and place of residence of every shipper and consignee, together with the quantity of goods, wares or merchandize shipped by and to each; and upon the oath or affirmation of the said master before the said collector or surveyor to the truth of such manifest, and that he doth not know, and hath no reason to believe that the revenue of the United States has been defrauded of any part of the duties imposed by law upon the importations of any of the goods, wares or merchandize contained in the said manifest, it shall be the duty of such collector or surveyor to return to the said master one of the said manifests, first certifying thereon that the same had been sworn or affirmed to, and delivered to him according to law, and also to grant to the said master a permit authorising such ship or vessel to proceed to the place of her destination. *And make oath thereto. Collector to return one manifest & grant a permit.*

So always and provided, That where goods, wares, or merchandizes of foreign growth or manufacture, are to be transported to and from the respective ports of Philadelphia and Baltimore unto each other, through and across the state of Delaware, a manifest certified as aforesaid by the officers of that one of the said ports from whence the same goods, wares or merchandizes are to be so transported, shall be sufficient to warrant the transportation thereof to the other of the said ports, without an intermediate entry in the district of Delaware. *Goods transported from and to Philadelphia & Baltimore across the state of Delaware, to be accompanied with a manifest.*

Provided always, That no master of any ship or vessel, licenced to trade as aforesaid, having on board goods, wares or merchandize of the growth,

[98]

Vessels licenced may proceed from district to district without manifest or permit.

or manufacture of the United States only, rum and other ardent spirits exceeding four hundred gallons excepted, and being bound from one district to another in the same state, or from a district in one state to a district in the next adjoining state shall be obliged to deliver duplicate manifests, or to apply for a permit as aforesaid; but any such master may in such case lawfully proceed to any other district in the same state, or in the next adjoining state, freely and without interruption.

Or having on board goods, &c. of growth or manufacture of the U. States & bound to a district in any other than an adjoining state the master must deliver duplicate manifests, &c.

Sec. 26. *And be it further enacted*, That the master of every ship or vessel of the burthen of twenty tons or upwards, licenced to trade as aforesaid having on board goods, wares or merchandize of the growth or manufacture of the United States only, and being bound from a district in one state to a district in any other than an adjoining state shall deliver to the collector, or where the collector and surveyor reside at different places within the same district, to the collector or surveyor as the one or the other may reside at or nearest to the port where such ship or vessel may be, duplicate manifests of the whole cargo on board such ship or vessel, specifying therein the name and place of residence of every shipper and consignee, together with the quantity of goods, wares or merchandize shipped by and to each: And upon the oath or affirmation of the said master, before the said collector or surveyor, to the truth of such manifest, it shall be the duty of such collector or surveyor to return to the said master one of the said manifests, first certifying thereon, that the same had been sworn or affirmed to and delivered to him according to law, and also to grant to the said master a permit, authorising such ship or vessel to proceed to the place of her destination.

On oath, and obtain a permit.

Sec. 27. *And be it further enacted*, That the master of every ship or vessel of the burthen of twenty tons or upwards, licenfed to trade as aforefaid, not having on board rum or other ardent fpirits, exceeding four hundred gallons, and arriving from one diftrict to another in the fame ftate, or from a diftrict in one ftate to a diftrict in the next adjoining ftate, with goods, wares or merchandize, of the growth or manufacture of the United States only, fhall, within twenty-four hours, Sundays excepted, next after his arrival at any place or port where a collector or furveyor refides, and before any part of the cargo on board fuch fhip or veffel be landed or unloaded, deliver to fuch collector or furveyor a manifeft thereof, and fhall make oath or affirmation before fuch collector or furveyor, that fuch manifeft contains a true account of all the goods, wares and merchandize on board fuch fhip or veffel, and thereupon fhall receive from fuch collector or furveyor a permit to land or unload the fame.

Arriving at the diftrict to which bound, muft deliver a manifeft, make oath and receive a permit.

Sec. 28. *And be it further enacted*, That in all other cafes the mafter of every veffel of the burthen of twenty tons or upwards, licenfed to trade as aforefaid, fhall within twenty-four hours, Sundays excepted, next after his arrival at any port or place within the United States, where a collector or furveyor refides, and before any part of the cargo on board any fuch fhip or veffel be landed or unloaded, deliver to fuch collector or furveyor the manifeft thereof, authenticated before and received from the collector or furveyor of the port or place where the faid cargo was taken on board, together with his permit to depart from the place of lading, whereupon it fhall be the duty of fuch collector or furveyor to grant a permit to land or unload fuch cargo.

In all other cafes mafter of licenfed veffel to deliver a manifeft & permit from the collector or furveyor where the cargo was taken on board.

Sec. 29. *And be it further enacted*, That if the mafter of any fhip or veffel, of the burthen of twenty tons or upwards, licenfed to trade as aforefaid, and having on board goods, wares or merchandize,

of the value of two hundred dollars, or upwards,
shall depart with the said ship or vessel from any
port, with intent to go to another district, without
such manifest and permit, except as is herein after
provided, the master or owner of such ship or vessel
shall forfeit and pay the sum of four hundred dollars for every such offence; and all goods, wares
and merchandize, of the value of two hundred
dollars or upwards, which shall be found on board
any such ship or vessel after her departure from the
port where the same were taken on board, without
being contained in, and accompanied with such
manifest as is herein before directed, except as is
herein after excepted, shall be subject to seizure and
forfeiture.

Provided always, That nothing herein contained
shall be construed to subject the master or owner of
any ship or vessel licenced to trade as aforesaid, having on board goods, wares and merchandize of
the growth and manufacture of the United States
only, rum and other ardent spririts exceeding four
hundred gallons, excepted, and bound from district
to district in the same state, or from a district in
one state to a district in the next adjoining state, to
any penalty for having departed from the port of
loading without such permit and manifest, or to
subject the said goods on board such ship or vessel
to seizure or forfeiture, in case they are not accompanied with a manifest as aforesaid.

Sec. 30. *And be it further enacted,* That if any
ship or vessel having a licence to trade or fish, for
one year, shall within that time be destined to any
foreign port, the master or commander of every
such ship or vessel, shall before he departs from
the United States, deliver such licence to the collector of the port from whence he intends to depart; and it shall be the duty of such collector
forthwith to transmit the licenfe to him so deli-

Marginalia:

Penalty on departing without manifest and permit.

Proviso.

Master of a licensed vessel bound to a foreign port must deliver up his licence.

vered, to the collector of the district where the same was granted, who shall thereupon cancel every licence; and if any master or commander shall neglect or refuse, to deliver up such licence before he depart from the United States, he shall forfeit and pay the sum of one hundred dollars for every such neglect or refusal.

Sec. 31. *And be it further enacted,* That the fees and allowances for the several duties to be performed in virtue of this act, and the distribution of the same, shall be as follows, to wit:— ^{Fees and allowances for the duties prescribed by this act.}

For the first register, or certificate of record granted for every ship or vessel, there shall be paid to the collector granting the same, the sum of two dollars.

For every subsequent one, one dollar and fifty cents.

For every certificate of enrollment, fifty cents.

For every licence to trade between the different districts of the United States, or to carry on the bank or whale fishery for one year, fifty cents.

For every entry of inward cargo directed to be made in conformity with this act, and for receiving of, and qualifying to every manifest of vessels licensed to trade as aforesaid, sixty cents.

For a permit to land goods of foreign growth or manufacture, twenty cents.

For every permit to proceed to the place of destination, twenty-five cents.

And for taking every bond required by this act, twenty cents.

The whole amount of which fees shall be accounted for by the collector, and where there is a collector, naval-officer and surveyor, shall be equally divided between the said officers, and ^{How to be distributed.}

where there is no naval-officer, between the collector and surveyor, and where there is only a collector, he shall receive the whole amount thereof, and where there is more than one surveyor in any district, each of them shall receive his proportionable part of such fees as shall arise in the port for which he is appointed. *Provided always*, That in all cases where the tonnage of any ship or vessel shall be ascertained by any person specially appointed for that purpose, as is herein before directed, that such person shall be allowed and paid by the collector a reasonable compensation for the same, out of the fees aforesaid, before any distribution thereof as aforesaid.

Naval officers to sign all official documents.

Sec. 32. *And be it further enacted*, That in every case where the collector is by this act directed to grant any licence, certificate, permit or other document, the naval-officer, if there be one residing at the port, shall sign the same.

In cases of forfeiture of goods or vessel, name of owner or consignee to be advertised.

Sec. 33. *And be it further enacted*, That in every case where a forfeiture of any ship or vessel, or of any goods, wares or merchandize shall accrue, it shall be the duty of the collector or other proper officer, who shall give notice of the sale of such ship or vessel, or of such goods, wares or merchandize, to insert in the same advertisement, the name or names, and the place or places of residence of the person or persons, to whom any such ship or vessel, goods, wares or merchandize, belonged or were consigned at the time of such seizure.

Penalties for offences against this act.

Sec. 34. *And be it further enacted*, That every collector who shall knowingly make any false register, record, or enrollment of any ship or vessel; and every officer or person appointed as is herein provided, who shall make any false record, or grant any false certificate, or any document whatever, in any manner that shall not be herein prescribed, or that shall be contrary to the true intent and meaning of this act, or shall take any other or greater fees than are by this act allowed, or receive any other reward or gratuity, contrary to the provisions of this act; and every surveyor, or other person appointed to measure ships or vessels, who shall wilfully deliver to any collector or naval-officer, a false description of any ship or vessel to be registered, recorded or enrolled, in pursuance of this act, shall, upon conviction of any such neglect or offence, forfeit the sum of one thousand dollars, and be rendered incapable of serving in any office of trust or profit under the United States; and if any person or persons, authorised and required by this act, in respect of his or their office, or offices, to perform any act or thing required to be done or performed, pursuant to any of the provisions of this act, and wilfully neglecting or refusing to do or perform the same, according to the true intent and meaning of this act, shall, on being duly convicted thereof, if not subject to the penalty and disqualification aforesaid, forfeit the sum of five hundred dollars for the first offence, and a like sum for the second offence, and shall from thence forward be rendered incapable of holding any office of trust or profit under the United States. *Penalties for offences against this act.*

Sec. 35. *And be it further enacted,* That if any certificate of registry, record, or enrollment, shall be fraudulently used for any ship or vessel, not entitled to the same by this act, such ship or vessel shall be forfeited to the United States, with her tackle, apparel and furniture. *Certificate of registry, &c. fraudulently used, ship or vessel forfeited.*

Sec. 36. *And be it further enacted,* That if any person or persons shall falsely make oath or affirmation to any of the matters herein required to be verified, such person or persons shall suffer the like pains and penalties, as shall be incurred by persons committing wilful and corrupt perjury; *Farther penalties for offences against this act.*

and that if any person or persons, shall forge, counterfeit, erase, alter or falsify, any certificate, register, licence, permit or other document, mentioned in this act, or to be granted by any officer of the customs, such person or persons shall, for every such offence, forfeit the sum of five hundred dollars.

<small>No allowance on exportation of dried or pickled fish, or salted provision, prior to the last day of May, 1790.</small>

Sec. 37. *And whereas*, By an act entitled, " An act for laying a duty on goods, wares and merchandizes imported into the United States," it is provided, That there shall be allowed or paid five cents on every quintal of dried fish, and on every barrel of pickled fish, and of salted provisions, exported from the United States to any country without the limits thereof, in lieu of the drawback of the duties imposed on the importation of the salt employed and expended therein, and there are now large quantities of salt within the United States, imported before any duties were laid for the use of the said States:

Be it enacted, That no allowance shall be made by any collector, for any dried or pickled fish, or for any salted provisions, which shall be exported from the United States prior to the last day of May, one thousand seven hundred and ninety.

FREDERICK AUGUSTUS MUHLENBERG,
Speaker of the House of Representatives.

JOHN ADAMS, *Vice-President of the United States, and President of the Senate.*

Approved, September the 1st, 1789.

GEORGE WASHINGTON,
President of the United States.

CHAPTER XII.

An ACT *to establish the* TREASURY DEPARTMENT.

Section 1. BE it enacted by the SENATE and HOUSE of REPRESENTATIVES of the United States of America in Congress assembled, That there shall be a department of Treasury, in which shall be the following officers, namely; a Secretary of the Treasury, to be deemed head of the department; a Comptroller, an Auditor, a Treasurer, a Register, and an Assistant to the Secretary of the Treasury, which Assistant shall be appointed by the said Secretary. *Department designated; officers therein.*

Sec. 2. *And be it further enacted,* That it shall be the duty of the Secretary of the Treasury to digest and prepare plans for the improvement and management of the revenue, and for the support of public credit; to prepare and report estimates of the public revenue, and the public expenditures; to superintend the collection of the revenue; to decide on the forms of keeping and stating accounts and making returns, and to grant under the limitations herein established, or to be hereafter provided, all warrants for monies to be issued from the Treasury, in pursuance of appropriations by law; to execute such services relative to the sale of the lands belonging to the United States, as may be by law required of him; to make report, and give information to either branch of the Legislature, in person or in writing (as he may be required), respecting all matters referred to him by the Senate or House of Representatives, or which shall appertain to his office; and generally to perform all such services relative to the finances, as he shall be directed to perform. *Duties of the secretary.*

Sec. 3. *And be it further enacted,* That it shall be the duty of the Comptroller to superintend the adjustment and preservation of the public accounts; to examine all accounts settled by the Auditor, and *Duties of the comptroller.*

Duties of the comptroller;

certify the balances arifing thereon to the Regifter ; to counterfign all warrants drawn by the Secretary of the Treafury, which fhall be warranted by law ; to report to the Secretary the official forms of all papers to be iffued in the different offices for collecting the public revenue, and the manner and form of keeping and ftating the accounts of the feveral perfons employed therein : He fhall moreover provide for the regular and punctual payment of all monies which may be collected, and fhall direct profecutions for all delinquencies of officers of the revenue, and for debts that are, or fhall be due to the United States.

Of the treafurer.

Sec. 4. *And be it further enacted*, That it fhall be the duty of the Treafurer to receive and keep the monies of the United States, and to difburfe the fame upon warrants drawn by the Secretary of the Treafury, counterfigned by the Comptroller recorded by the Regifter, and not otherwife ; he fhall take receipts for all monies paid by him, and all receipts for monies received by him, fhall be endorfed upon warrants figned by the Secretary of the Treafury, without which warrant fo figned, no acknowledgment for money received into the public treafury fhall be valid. And the faid Treafurer fhall render his accounts to the Comptroller quarterly (or oftener if required), and fhall tranfmit a copy thereof, when fettled, to the Secretary of the Treafury. He fhall moreover, on the third day of every feffion of Congrefs, lay before the Senate and Houfe of Reprefentatives, fair and accurate copies of all accounts by him from time to time rendered to, and fettled with the Comptroller as aforefaid, as alfo, a true and perfect account of the ftate of the Treafury. He fhall at all times fubmit to the Secretary of the Treafury, and the Comptroller, or either of them, the infpection of the monies in his hands ; and fhall, prior to the entering upon the duties of his office, give bond, with sufficient sureties, to be approved by the Secretary of the Treasury and Comptroller, in the sum of one hundred and fifty thousand dollars, payable to the United States, with condition for the faithful performance of the duties of his office, and for the fidelity of the persons to be by him employed, which bond shall be lodged in the office of the Comptroller of the Treasury of the United States. Duties of the treasurer;

Sec. 5. *And be it further enacted,* That it shall be the duty of the Auditor to receive all public accounts, and after examination to certify the balance, and transmit the accounts with the vouchers and certificate to the Comptroller for his decision thereon: *Provided,* That if any person whose account shall be so audited, be dissatisfied therewith, he may within six months appeal to the Comptroller against such settlement. Of the auditor;

Sec. 6. *And be it further enacted,* That it shall be the duty of the Register to keep all accounts of the receipts and expenditures of the public money, and of all debts due to or from the United States ; to receive from the Comptroller the accounts which shall have been finally adjusted, and to preserve such accounts with their vouchers and certificates ; to record all warrants for the receipt or payment of monies at the treasury, certify the same thereon, and to transmit to the Secretary of the Treasury, copies of the certificates of balances of accounts adjusted as is herein directed. Of the register.

Sec. 7. *And be it further enacted,* That whenever the Secretary shall be removed from office by the President of the United States, or in any other case of vacancy in the office of Secretary, the assistant shall, during the vacancy, have the charge and custody of the records, books, and papers appertaining to the said office. Secretary removed, or his office vacant, assistant to have custody of records, &c.

Sec. 8. *And be it further enacted,* That no person appointed to any office instituted by this act, shall directly or indirectly be concerned or interested in carrying on the business of trade or commerce, or be owner in whole or in part of any sea vessel, or purchase by himself, or another in trust for him, public lands or any other public property, or be concerned in the purchase or disposal of any public securities of any state, or of the United States, or take or apply to his own use, any emolument or gain for negociating or transacting any business in the said department, other than what shall be allowed by law ; and if any person shall offend against any of the prohibitions of this act, he shall be deemed guilty of a high misdemeanor, and forfeit to the United States the penalty of three thousand dollars, and shall upon conviction be removed from office, and forever thereafter incapable of holding any office under the United States : *Provided,* That if any other person than a public prosecutor shall give information of any such offence, upon which a prosecution and conviction shall be had, one half the aforesaid penalty of three thousand dollars when recovered, shall be for the use of the person giving such information.

[Marginalia: Persons appointed to office under this act, prohibition upon, And penalty for breach of them.]

FREDERICK AUGUSTUS MUHLENBERG,
Speaker of the House of Representatives.

JOHN ADAMS, *Vice-President of the United States.
and President of the Senate.*

Approved, September the 2d, 1789.

GEORGE WASHINGTON,
President of the United States.

CHAPTER XIII.

An ACT *for establishing the* SALARIES *of the* EXECUTIVE OFFICERS *of* GOVERNMENT, *with their* ASSISTANTS *and* CLERKS.

Section 1. **B**E *it enacted by the* SENATE *and* HOUSE *of* REPRESENTATIVES *of the United States of America in Congress assembled,* That there shall be allowed to the Officers hereafter mentioned, the following annual salaries, payable quarterly at the treasury of the United States: To the Secretary of the Treasury, three thousand five hundred dollars: To the Secretary in the department of state, three thousand five hundred dollars: To the Secretary in the department of war, three thousand dollars: To the comptroller of the treasury, two thousand dollars: To the auditor, fifteen hundred dollars: To the treasurer, two thousand dollars: To the register, twelve hundred and fifty dollars: To the governor of the western territory, for his salary as such, and for discharging the duties of superintendant of Indian affairs in the northern department, two thousand dollars: To the three judges of the western territory each, eight hundred dollars: To the assistant of the secretary of the treasury, fifteen hundred dollars: To the chief clerk in the department of state, eight hundred dollars: To the chief clerk in the department of war, six hundred dollars: To the secretary of the western territory, seven hundred and fifty dollars: To the principal clerk of the comptroller, eight hundred dollars: To the principal clerk of the auditor, six hundred dollars: To the principal clerk of the treasurer, six hundred dollars.

Annual salaries established, payable quarterly:

rate of, and to what officers allowed.

Sec. 2. *And be it further enacted,* That the heads of the three departments first above mentioned, shall appoint such clerks therein respectively as they shall

Heads of departments to appoint clerks;

<small>their sala-</small> find necessary; and the salary of the said clerks
<small>ries.</small> respectively shall not exceed the rate of five hundred
dollars per annum.

FREDERICK AUGUSTUS MUHLENBERG,
Speaker of the House of Representatives.

JOHN ADAMS, *Vice-President of the United States,
and President of the Senate.*

APPROVED, September the 11th, 1789.

GEORGE WASHINGTON,
President of the United States.

CHAPTER. XIV.

An ACT *to provide for the safe-keeping of the*
ACTS, RECORDS, *and* SEAL *of the United States,
and for other Purposes.*

<small>Department of foreign affairs changed to the department of state.</small> Section 1. **B**E *it enacted by the* SENATE *and* HOUSE *of* REPRESENTATIVES *of the United States of America in Congress assembled,* That the Executive Department, denominated the Department of Foreign Affairs, shall hereafter be denominated the Department of State, and the principal officer therein shall hereafter be called the Secretary of State.

<small>Additional duties assigned the secretary of the said department.</small> Sec. 2. *And be it further enacted,* That whenever a bill, order, resolution, or vote of the Senate and House of Representatives, having been approved and signed by the President of the United States, or not having been returned by him with his objections, shall become a law, or take effect, it shall forthwith thereafter be received by the said Secretary from the President : and whenever a bill, order, resolution, or vote, shall be returned by the President with his objections, and shall, on being reconsidered, be agreed to be passed, and be ap-

proved by two thirds of both Houfes of Congrefs, and thereby become a law or take effect, it fhall, in fuch cafe, be received by the faid Secretary from the Prefident of the Senate, or the Speaker of the Houfe of Reprefentatives, in whichfoever Houfe it fhall laft have been fo approved; and the faid Secretary fhall, as foon as conveniently may be, after he fhall receive the fame, caufe every fuch law, order, refolution, and vote, to be publifhed in at leaft three of the public newfpapers printed within the United States, and fhall alfo caufe one printed copy to be delivered to each Senator and Reprefentative of the United States, and two printed copies duly authenticated to be fent to the executive authority of each ftate; and he fhall carefully preferve the originals, and fhall caufe the fame to be recorded in books to be provided for the purpofe.

Sec. 3. *And be it further enacted,* That the feal heretofore ufed by the United States in Congrefs affembled, fhall be, and hereby is declared to be the feal of the United States. Seal of the United States.

Sec. 4. *And be it further enacted,* That the faid Secretary fhall keep the faid feal, and fhall make out and record, and fhall affix the faid feal to all civil commiffions, to officers of the United States, to be appointed by the Prefident by and with the advice and confent of the Senate, or by the Prefident alone. *Provided,* That the faid feal fhall not be affixed to any commiffion, before the fame fhall have been figned by the Prefident of the United States, nor to any other inftrument or act, without the fpecial warrant of the Prefident therefor. Secretary to keep and affix the feal to all civil commiffions.

Sec. 5. *And be it further enacted,* That the faid Secretary fhall caufe a feal of office to be made for the faid department of fuch device as the Prefident of the United States fhall approve, and all copies Secretary to provide a feal of office, of records and papers in the said office, authenticated under the said seal, shall be evidence equally as the original record or paper.

Fees of office to be paid for the use of the United States.

Sec. 6. *And be it further enacted*, That there shall be paid to the Secretary, for the use of the United States, the following fees of office, by the persons requiring the services to be performed, except when they are performed for any officer of the United States, in a matter relating to the duties of his office, to wit: For making out and authenticating copies of records, ten cents for each sheet, containing one hundred words; for authenticating a copy of a record or paper under the seal of office, twenty-five cents.

Secretary to have custody of papers, &c. of late Congress.

Sec. 7. *And be it further enacted*, That the said Secretary shall forthwith after his appointment, be entitled to have the custody and charge of the said seal of the United States, and also of all books, records and papers, remaining in the office of the late Secretary of the United States in Congress assembled; and such of the said books, records and papers, as may appertain to the Treasury department, or War department, shall be delivered over to the principal officers in the said departments respectively, as the President of the United States shall direct.

FREDERICK AUGUSTUS MUHLENBERG,
Speaker of the House of Representatives.

JOHN ADAMS, *Vice-President of the United States.*
and President of the Senate.

APPROVED, September the 15th, 1789.

GEORGE WASHINGTON,
President of the United States.

CHAPTER XV.

An ACT *to suspend part of an Act, entitled " An Act to regulate the collection of the* Duties *imposed by Law on the Tonnage of* Ships *or* Vessels, *and on* Goods, Wares, *and* Merchandizes, *imported into the United States," and for other Purposes.*

Section 1. BE *it enacted by the* Senate *and* House *of* Representatives *of the United States of America in Congress assembled*, That so much of the act, entitled " An Act to regulate the collection of the duties imposed by law, on the tonnage of ships or vessels, and on goods, wares, and merchandizes, imported into the United States," as obliges ships or vessels bound up the river Potowmac, to come to, and deposit manifests of their cargoes, with the officers at Saint Mary's and Yeocomico, before they proceed to their port of delivery, shall be and is hereby suspended until the first day of May next.

^{Restriction on vessels bound up the Potowmac suspended.}

Sec. 2. *Be it further enacted*, That all the privileges and advantages to which ships and vessels owned by citizens of the United States, are by law entitled, shall be, until the fifteenth day of January next, extended to ships and vessels wholly owned by citizens of the States of North-Carolina, and Rhode-Island and Providence Plantations.— *Provided*, That the master of every such ship or vessel last mentioned, shall produce a register for the same, conformable to the laws of the state in which it shall have been obtained, shewing that the said ship or vessel is, and before the first day of September instant, was owned as aforesaid, and make oath or affirmation, before the collector of the port in which the benefit of this act is claimed, that the ship or vessel for which such register is produced, is the same therein mentioned, and that he believes it is still wholly owned by the person or

^{Privileges of ships &c. of the United States extended to ships, &c. of North Carolina and Rhode-Island, until the 15th of January next.}

persons named in said register, and that he or they are citizens of one of the states aforesaid.

<small>Certain articles subject to duties as on foreign goods.</small>

Sec. 3. *And be it further enacted,* That all rum, loaf sugar, and chocolate, manufactured or made in the States of North-Carolina, or Rhode-Island and Providence Plantations, and imported or brought into the United States, shall be deemed and taken to be, subject to the like duties, as goods of the like kinds, imported from any foreign state, kingdom or country, are made subject to.

<small>Rehoboth established a port of entry.</small>

Sec. 4. *And be it further enacted,* That Rehoboth, in the state of Massachusetts, shall be a port of entry and delivery, until the fifteenth day of January next, and that a collector be appointed for the same.

FREDERICK AUGUSTUS MUHLENBERG
Speaker of the House of Representatives.

JOHN ADAMS, *Vice-President of the United States and President of the Senate.*

APPROVED, September the 16th, 1789.

GEORGE WASHINGTON
President of the United States.

CHAPTER XVI.

An ACT *for the temporary establishment of the* POST OFFICE.

<small>Powers and salary.</small>

Section 1. BE *it enacted by the* SENATE *and* HOUSE *of* REPRESENTATIVES *of the United States of America in Congress assembled,* That there shall be appointed a Postmaster-general; his powers and salary, and the compensation to the assistant or clerk and deputies which he may appoint, and the regulations of the post-office shall

be the same as they last were under the resolutions and ordinances of the late Congress. The Postmaster-general to be subject to the direction of the President of the United States in performing the duties of his office, and in forming contracts for the transportation of the mail.

Sec. 2. *Be it further enacted*, That this act shall continue in force until the end of the next session of Congress, and no longer.

<small>Limitation.</small>

FREDERICK AUGUSTUS MUHLENBERG,
Speaker of the House of Representatives.
JOHN ADAMS, *Vice-President of the United States, and President of the Senate.*
APPROVED, September the 18th, 1789.
GEORGE WASHINGTON,
President of the United States.

CHAPTER XVII.

An ACT *for allowing* COMPENSATION *to the Members of the Senate and House of Representatives of the United States, and to the Officers of both Houses.*

Section 1. BE *it enacted by the* SENATE *and* HOUSE *of* REPRESENTATIVES *of the United States of America in Congress assembled,* That at every session of Congress, and at every meeting of the Senate in the recess of Congress, prior to the fourth day of March, in the year one thousand seven hundred and ninety-five, each Senator shall be entitled to receive six dollars, for every day he shall attend the Senate, and shall also be allowed, at the commencement and end of every such session and meeting, six dollars for every twenty miles of the estimated distance, by the most usual road, from his place of residence to the seat of Con-

<small>Senators, their allowance for attendance & travelling, prior to the 4th of March, 1795.</small>

gress: And in case any member of the Senate shall be detained by sickness on his journey to or from any such session or meeting, or after his arrival shall be unable to attend the Senate, he shall be entitled to the same daily allowance: *Provided always,* That no Senator shall be allowed a sum exceeding the rate of six dollars a day, from the end of one such session or meeting to the time of his taking a seat in another.

<small>Allowance for attendance & travelling, after the 4th of March, 1795.</small>

Sec. 2. *And be it further enacted,* That at every session of Congress, and at every meeting of the Senate in the recess of Congress, after the aforesaid fourth day of March, in the year one thousand seven hundred and ninety-five, each Senator shall be entitled to receive seven dollars for every day he shall attend the Senate; and shall also be allowed at the commencement and end of every such session and meeting, seven dollars for every twenty miles of the estimated distance, by the most usual road, from his place of residence to the seat of Congress And in case any member of the Senate shall be detained by sickness, on his journey to or from any such session or meeting, or after his arrival shall be unable to attend the Senate, he shall be entitled to the same allowance of seven dollars a day: *Provided always,* That no Senator shall be allowed a sum exceeding the rate of seven dollars a day, from the end of one such session or meeting to the time of his taking a seat in another.

<small>Members of the House of Representatives, their allowance for attendance and travelling.</small>

Sec. 3. *And be it further enacted,* That at every session of Congress, each Representative shall be entitled to receive six dollars for every day he shall attend the House of Representatives; and shall also be allowed at the commencement and end of every session, six dollars for every twenty miles of the estimated distance, by the most usual road, from his place of residence to the seat of Congress: And in case any Representative shall be detained by sickness, on his journey to or from the session of Con-

gress, or after his arrival shall be unable to attend the House of Representatives, he shall be entitled to the daily allowance aforesaid: And the Speaker of the House of Representatives, to defray the incidental expenses of his office, shall be entitled to receive in addition to his compensation as a Representative, six dollars for every day he shall attend the House: *Provided always,* That no Representative shall be allowed a sum exceeding the rate of six dollars a day, from the end of one such session or meeting to the time of his taking a seat in another.

Sec. 4. *And be it further enacted,* That there shall be allowed to each chaplain of Congress, at the rate of five hundred dollars per annum during the session of Congress; to the secretary of the Senate and clerk of the House of Representatives, fifteen hundred dollars per annum each, to commence from the time of their respective appointments; and also a further allowance of two dollars per day to each, during the session of that branch for which he officiates: And the said secretary and clerk shall each be allowed (when the President of the Senate or Speaker shall deem it necessary) to employ one principal clerk, who shall be paid three dollars per day, and an engrossing clerk, who shall be paid two dollars per day during the session, with the like compensation to such clerk while he shall be necessarily employed in the recess. *[Chaplains, secretary & clerks, their salaries and allowance.]*

Sec. 5. *And be it further enacted,* That the following compensation shall be allowed to the officers hereinafter mentioned, viz. To the serjeant at arms, during the sessions and while employed on the business of the House, four dollars per day; the allowance of the present serjeant at arms to commence from the time of his appointment: To the door-keeper of the Senate and House of Representatives, for their services in those offices, three dollars per day during the session of the House to which *[Serjeant at arms, and door-keepers; their allowance for services, attendance, &c.]*

[118]

he may belong, for his own services, and for the hire of necessary labourers; the allowance to the present door-keeper of the Senate to commence from the day appointed for the meeting of Congress; and the allowance to the door-keeper of the House of Representatives to commence from his appointment; and to the assistant door-keeper to each House, two dollars per day during the sessions.

<small>Compensations, how to be certified.</small>

Sec. 6. *And be it further enacted,* That the said compensation which shall be due to the members and officers of the Senate, shall be certified by the President; and that which shall be due to the members and officers of the House of Representatives, shall be certified by the Speaker; and the same shall be passed as public accounts, and paid out of the public treasury.

<small>Continuance of this act.</small>

Sec. 7. *And be it further enacted,* That this act shall continue in force until the fourth day of March, in the year one thousand seven hundred and ninety-six, and no longer.

FREDERICK AUGUSTUS MUHLENBERG,
Speaker of the House of Representatives.

JOHN ADAMS, *Vice-President of the United States, and President of the Senate.*

APPROVED, September the 22d, 1789.

GEORGE WASHINGTON,
President of the United States.

CHAPTER XVIII.

An ACT *for allowing certain* COMPENSATION *to the* Judges *of the* Supreme *and other* Courts, *and to the* Attorney-General *of the* United States.

Section 1. BE *it enacted by the* SENATE *and* HOUSE *of* REPRESENTATIVES *of the United States of America in Congress assembled,* That there shall be allowed to the judges of the supreme and other courts of the United States, the yearly compensations herein after mentioned, to wit; to the chief justice four thousand dollars; to each of the justices of the supreme court three thousand five hundred dollars; to the judge of the district of Maine one thousand dollars; to the judge of the district of New-Hampshire one thousand dollars; to the judge of the district of Massachusetts twelve hundred dollars; to the judge of the district of Connecticut one thousand dollars; to the judge of the district of New-York fifteen hundred dollars; to the judge of the district of New-Jersey one thousand dollars; to the judge of the district of Pennsylvania sixteen hundred dollars; to the judge of the district of Delaware eight hundred dollars; to the judge of the district of Maryland fifteen hundred dollars; to the judge of the district of Virginia eighteen hundred dollars; to the judge of the district of Kentucky one thousand dollars; to the judge of the district of South-Carolina eighteen hundred dollars; to the judge of the district of Georgia fifteen hundred dollars; and to the attorney-general of the United States fifteen hundred dollars; which compensations shall commence from their respective appointments, and be paid at the treasury of the United States in quarterly payments.

Salaries of chief justice, justices of the supreme court, and district judges.

Commencement of, and how payable.

FREDERICK AUGUSTUS MUHLENBERG,
Speaker of the House of Representatives.

JOHN ADAMS, *Vice-President of the United States,*
and President of the Senate.

APPROVED, September the 23d, 1789.

GEORGE WASHINGTON,
President of the United States.

CHAPTER XIX.

An ACT *for allowing a* COMPENSATION *to the* PRESIDENT *and* VICE-PRESIDENT *of the United States.*

<small>President & Vice-President of the U. States, compensation to, commencement of, and how payable.</small>

Section 1. BE it enacted by the SENATE and HOUSE of REPRESENTATIVES of the United States of America in Congress assembled, That there shall be allowed to the President of the United States, at the rate of twenty-five thousand dollars, with the use of the furniture and other effects, now in his possession, belonging to the United States; and to the Vice-President, at the rate of five thousand dollars per annum, in full compensation for their respective services, to commence with the time of their entering on the duties of their offices respectively, and to continue so long as they shall remain in office, and to be paid quarterly out of the treasury of the United States.

FREDERICK AUGUSTUS MUHLENBERG,
Speaker of the House of Representatives.

JOHN ADAMS, *Vice-President of the United States, and President of the Senate.*

APPROVED, September the 24th, 1789.

GEORGE WASHINGTON,
President of the United States.

CHAPTER XX.

An ACT *to establish the* JUDICIAL COURTS *of the United States.*

<small>Supreme court, chief justice, five associates.</small>

Section 1. BE it enacted by the SENATE and HOUSE of REPRESENTATIVES of the United States of America in Congress assembled, That the supreme court of the United States shall consist of a chief justice and five associate justices, any four of whom shall be a quorum, and shall

<small>Two sessions annually.</small>

hold annually at the seat of government two sessions, the one commencing the first Monday of

[121]

February, and the other the first Monday of August. That the associate justices shall have precedence according to the date of their commissions, or when the commissions of two or more of them bear date on the same day, according to their respective ages.

Sec. 2. *And be it further enacted*, That the United States shall be, and they hereby are divided into thirteen districts, to be limited and called as follows, to wit, one to consist of that part of the state of Massachusetts which lies easterly of the state of New-Hampshire, and to be called Main District; one to consist of the state of New-Hampshire, and to be called New-Hampshire District; one to consist of the remaining part of the state of Massachusetts, and to be called Massachusetts District; one to consist of the state of Connecticut, and to be called Connecticut District; one to consist of the state of New-York, and to be called New-York District; one to consist of the state of New-Jersey, and to be called New-Jersey District; one to consist of the state of Pennsylvania, and to be called Pennsylvania District; one to consist of the state of Delaware, and to be called Delaware District; one to consist of the state of Maryland, and to be called Maryland District; one to consist of the state of Virginia, except that part called the District of Kentucky, and to be called Virginia District; one to consist of the remaining part of the state of Virginia, and to be called Kentucky District; one to consist of the state of South-Carolina, and to be called the South-Carolina District; and one to consist of the state of Georgia, and to be called Georgia District. *Thirteen districts. Their divisions.*

Sec. 3. *And be it further enacted*, That there be a court called a District Court, in each of the aforementioned districts, to consist of one judge, who shall reside in the district for which he is appointed, and shall be called a District Judge, and shall *A district court in each district.*

[122]

<small>Four feffions annually in a diftrict; and when held.</small> hold annually four feffions, the firft of which t commence as follows, to wit, in the diftricts c New-York and of New-Jerfey on the firft, in th diftrict of Pennfylvania on the fecond, in the di: trict of Connecticut on the third, and in the diftric of Delaware, on the fourth Tuefdays of Novembe next ; in the diftricts of Maffachufetts, of Main and of Maryland, on the firft ; in the diftrict c Georgia on the fecond, and in the diftricts of New Hampfhire, of Virginia, and of Kentucky, on th third Tuefdays of December next ; and the othe three feffions progreffively in the refpective di tricts on the like Tuefdays of every third calenda month afterwards, and in the diftrict of Soutl Carolina, on the third Monday in March and Sep tember, the firft Monday in July, and the fecon Monday of December of each and every year, con

<small>Special diftrict courts.</small> mencing in December next ; and that the Diftric Judge fhall have power to hold fpecial courts at hi difcretion. That the ftated diftrict court fhall b held at the places following, to wit, in the diftric of Main, at Portland and Pownalborough alte: nately, beginning at the firft ; in the diftrict c New-Hampfhire, at Exeter and Portfmouth alte: nately, beginning at the firft ; in the diftrict c Maffachufetts, at Bofton and Salem alternately, be ginning at the firft ; in the diftrict of Connecticu alternately at Hartford and New-Haven, beginnin at the firft ; in the diftrict of New-York, at New York ; in the diftrict of New-Jerfey, alternately a New-Brunfwick and Burlington, beginning at th firft ; in the diftrict of Pennfylvania, at Philadelphi and York-Town alternately, beginning at the firft in the diftrict of Delaware, alternately at Newcaftl and Dover, beginning at the firft ; in the diftrict o Maryland, alternately at Baltimore and Eafton, be ginning at the firft ; in the diftrict of Virginia, al ternately at Richmond and Williamfburgh, begin ning at the firft ; in the diftrict of Kentucky, a

[123]

Harrodsburgh; in the district of South-Carolina, at Charleston; and in the district of Georgia, alternately at Savannah and Augusta, beginning at the first;—and that the special courts shall be held at the same place in each district as the stated courts, or in districts that have two, at either of them, in the discretion of the judge, or at such other place in the district, as the nature of the business and his discretion shall direct. And that in the districts that have but one place for holding the district court, the records thereof shall be kept at that place; and in districts that have two, at that place in each district which the judge shall appoint. *Special courts, where held.* *Where records kept.*

Sec. 4. *And be it further enacted,* That the beforementioned districts, except those of Maine and Kentucky, shall be divided into three circuits, and be called the eastern, the middle and the southern circuit. That the eastern circuit shall consist of the districts of New-Hampshire, Massachusetts, Connecticut and New-York; that the middle circuit shall consist of the districts of New-Jersey, Pennsylvania, Delaware, Maryland and Virginia; and that the southern circuit shall consist of the districts of South-Carolina and Georgia, and that there shall be held annually in each district of said circuits, two courts, which shall be called Circuit Courts, and shall consist of any two justices of the supreme court, and the district judge of such districts, any two of whom shall constitute a quorum: *Provided,* That no district judge shall give a vote in any case of appeal or error from his own decision; but may sign the reasons of such his decision. *Three circuits, & how divided.*

Sec. 5. *And be it further enacted,* That the first session of the said circuit court in the several districts shall commence at the times following, to wit; in New-Jersey on the second, in New-York on the fourth, in Pennsylvania on the eleventh in Connecticut on the twenty-second, and in Delaware on *First session of the circuit courts.*

<small>First session of the circuit courts.</small> the twenty-seventh days of April next; in Massachusetts on the third, in Maryland on the seventh, in South-Carolina on the twelfth, in New-Hampshire on the twentieth, in Virginia on the twenty-second, and in Georgia on the twenty-eighth days of May next, and the subsequent sessions in the respective districts on the like days of every sixth calendar month afterwards, except in South-Carolina, where the session of the said court shall commence on the first, and in Georgia where it shall commence on the seventeenth day of October, and except when any of those days shall happen on a Sunday, and then the session shall commence on the next day following. And the sessions of the said circuit court shall be held in the district of New-Hampshire, at Portsmouth and Exeter alternately, beginning at the first; in the district of Massachusetts at Boston; in the district of Connecticut, alternately at Hartford and New-Haven, beginning at the last; in the district of New-York, alternately at New-York and Albany, beginning at the first; in the district of New-Jersey, at Trenton; in the district of Pennsylvania, alternately at Philadelphia and York-Town, beginning at the first; in the district of Delaware, alternately at Newcastle and Dover, beginning at the first; in the district of Maryland, alternately at Annapolis and Easton, beginning at the first; in the district of Virginia, alternately at Charlottesville and Williamsburgh, beginning at the first; in the district of South-Carolina, alternately at Columbia and Charleston, beginning at the first; and in the district of Georgia, alternately at Savannah and Augusta, beginning at the first.

<small>Circuit courts. Special sessions.</small> And the circuit courts shall have power to hold special sessions for the trial of criminal causes at any other time at their discretion, or at the discretion of the supreme court.

Sec. 6. *And be it further enacted*, That the supreme court may, by any one or more of its jus-

tices being present, be adjourned from day to day until a quorum be convened; and that a circuit court may also be adjourned from day to day by any one of its judges, or if none are present, by the marshal of the district until a quorum be convened; and that a district court, in case of the inability of the judge to attend at the commencement of a session, may by virtue of a written order from the said judge directed to the marshal of the district, be adjourned by the said marshal to such day, antecedent to the next stated session of the said court, as in the said order shall be appointed, and in case of the death of the said judge, and his vacancy not being supplied, all process, pleadings and proceedings of what nature soever, pending before the said court, shall be continued of course until the next stated session after the appointment and acceptance of the office by his successor.

Supreme court adjourned by one or more justices, circuit courts adjourned.

District courts adjourned.

Sec. 7. *And be it enacted,* That the supreme court, and the district courts shall have power to appoint clerks for their respective courts, and that the clerk for each district court shall be clerk also of the circuit court in such district, and each of the said clerks shall, before he enters upon the execution of his office, take the following oath or affirmation, to wit; " I, A. B. being appointed clerk of
' do solemnly swear, or affirm, that I will truly and
' faithfully enter and record all the orders, de-
' crees, judgments and proceedings of the said
' court, and that I will faithfully and impartially
' discharge and perform all the duties of my said
' office, according to the best of my abilities and
' understanding. So help me God." Which words, so help me God, shall be omitted in all cases where an affirmation is admitted instead of an oath. And the said clerks shall also severally give bond, with sufficient sureties, (to be approved of by the supreme and districts courts respectively) to

The courts have power to appoint clerks.

Their oath or affirmation.

the United States, in the sum of two thousand dollars, faithfully to discharge the duties of his office, and seasonably to record the decrees, judgments and determinations of the court of which he is clerk

Oath of justices of supreme court & judges of the district court.

Sec. 8. *And be it further enacted,* That the justices of the supreme court, and the district judges, before they proceed to execute the duties of their respective offices, shall take the following oath or affirmation, to wit ; " I, A. B. do solemnly swear or affirm, that I will administer justice without respect to persons, and do equal right to the poor and to the rich, and that I will faithfully and impartially discharge and perform all the duties incumbent on me as   , according to the best of my abilities and understanding, agreeably to the constitution and laws of the United States. So help me God."

District courts exclusive jurisdiction.

Sec. 9. *And be it further enacted,* That the district courts shall have, exclusively of the courts of the several states, cognizance of all crimes and offences that shall be cognizable under the authority of the United States, committed within their respective districts, or upon the high seas ; where no other punishment than whipping, not exceeding thirty stripes, a fine not exceeding one hundred dollars, or a term of imprisonment not exceeding six months, is to be inflicted ; and shall

Original cognizance in maritime causes & of seizure under the laws of the United States.

also have exclusive original cognizance of all civil causes of admiralty and maritime jurisdiction, including all seizures under laws of impost, navigation or trade of the United States, where the seizures are made, on waters which are navigable from the sea by vessels of ten or more tons burthen, within their respective districts as well as upon the high seas ; saving to suitors, in all cases, the right of a common law remedy, where the common law is competent to give it : And shall also have exclusive original cognizance of all seizure on land, or other waters than as aforesaid, made, and of all suits for penalties and forfeitures incurred, under the laws of the United States. And shall also have cognizance, concurrent with the courts of the several states, or the circuit courts, as the case may be, of all causes where an alien sues for a tort only in violation of the law of nations or a treaty of the United States. And shall also have cognizance, concurrent as last mentioned, of all suits at common law where the United States sue, and the matter in dispute amounts, exclusive of costs, to the sum or value of one hundred dollars. And shall also have jurisdiction exclusively of the courts of the several states, of all suits against consuls or vice-consuls, except for offences above the description aforesaid. And the trial of issues in fact, in the districts courts, in all causes except civil causes of admiralty and maritime jurisdiction, shall be by jury.

<small>Concurrent jurisdiction.</small>

<small>Trial of fact by jury.</small>

Sec. 10. *And be it further enacted,* That the district court in Kentucky district shall, besides the jurisdiction aforesaid, have jurisdiction of all other causes, except of appeals and writs of error, herein after made cognizable in a circuit court, and shall proceed therein in the same manner as a circuit court, and writs of error and appeals shall lie from decisions therein to the supreme court in the same causes, as from a circuit court to the supreme court, and under the same regulations.— And the district court in Maine district, shall besides the jurisdiction herein before granted, have jurisdiction of all causes, except of appeals and writs of error herein after made cognizable in a circuit court, and shall proceed therein in the same manner as a circuit court : And writs of error shall lie from decisions therein to the circuit court in the district of Massachusetts in the same manner as from other district courts to their respective circuit courts.

<small>Kentucky district court.</small>

<small>Maine district court.</small>

Sec. 11. *And be it further enacted*, That the circuit courts shall have original cognizance, concurrent with the courts of the several states, of all suits of a civil nature at common law or in equity, where the matter in dispute exceeds, exclusive of costs, the sum or value of five hundred dollars, and the United States are plaintiffs, or petitioners; or an alien is a party, or the suit is between a citizen of the state where the suit is brought, and a citizen of another state. And shall have exclusive cognizance of all crimes and offences cognizable under the authority of the United States, except where this act otherwise provides, or the laws of the United States shall otherwise direct, and concurrent jurisdiction with the district courts of the crimes and offences cognizable therein. But no person shall be arrested in one district for trial in another, in any civil action before a circuit or district court: And no civil suit shall be brought before either of said courts against an inhabitant of the United States, by any original process in any other district than that whereof he is an inhabitant, or in which he shall be found at the time of serving the writ, nor shall any district or circuit court have cognizance of any suit to recover the contents of any promissory note or other chose in action in favour of an assignee, unless a suit might have been prosecuted in such court to recover the said contents if no assignment had been made, except in cases of foreign bills of exchange. And the circuit courts shall also have appellate jurisdiction from the district courts under the regulations and restrictions herein after provided.

Sec. 12. *And be it further enacted*, That if a suit be commenced in any state court against an alien, or by a citizen of the state in which the suit is brought against a citizen of another state, and the matter in dispute exceeds the aforesaid sum or value of five hundred dollars, exclusive of costs, to be made to appear to the satisfaction of the court; and the defendant shall, at the time of entering his appearance in such state court, file a petition for the removal of the cause for trial into the next circuit court, to be held in the district where the suit is pending, or if in the district of Main to the district court next to be holden therein, or if in Kentucky district to the district court next to be holden therein, and offer good and sufficient surety for his entering in such court, on the first day of its session, copies of said process against him, and also for his there appearing and entering special bail in the cause, if special bail was originally requisite therein, it shall then be the duty of the state court to accept the surety, and proceed no further in the cause, and any bail that may have been originally taken shall be discharged, and the said copies being entered as aforesaid, in such court of the United States, the cause shall there proceed in the same manner as if it had been brought there by original process. And any attachment of the goods or estate of the defendant by the original process, shall hold the goods or estate so attached, to answer the final judgment in the same manner as by the laws of such state they would have been holden to answer final judgment, had it been rendered by the court in which the suit commenced. And if in any action commenced in a state court, the title of land be concerned, and the parties are citizens of the same state, and the matter in dispute exceeds the sum or value of five hundred dollars, exclusive of costs, the sum or value being made to appear to the satisfaction of the court, either party, before the trial, shall state to the court and make affidavit if they require it, that he claims and shall rely upon a right or title to the land, under a grant from a state, other than that in which the suit is pending, and produce the original grant or an exemplification of it, except where the loss

Special bail.

Attachment of goods holden to final judgment.

Title of land where value exceeds 500 dollars.

of public records shall put it out of his power, and shall move that the adverse party inform the court whether he claims a right or title to the land under a grant from the state in which the suit is pending the said adverse party shall give such information or otherwise not be allowed to plead such grant, or give it in evidence upon the trial, and if he inform that he does claim under such grant, the party claiming under the grant first mentioned, may then on motion, remove the cause for trial to the next

<small>If in Main and Kentucky, where causes are removeable.</small> circuit court to be holden in such district, or if in the district of Main, to the District court next to be holden therein; or if in Kentucky district, to the district court next to be holden therein; but if he is the defendant, shall do it under the same regulation as in the beforementioned case of the removal of cause into such court by an alien: And neither party removing the cause, shall be allowed to plead or give evidence of any other title than that by him stated as aforesaid, as the ground of his claim.

<small>Issues in fact by jury.</small> And the trial of issues in fact in the circuit court shall, in all suits, except those of equity, and of admiralty, and maritime jurisdiction, be by jury.

<small>Supreme court exclusive jurisdiction.</small> Sec. 13. *And be it further enacted,* That the supreme court shall have exclusive jurisdiction of all controversies of a civil nature, where a state is party, except between a state and its citizens; and except also between a state and citizens of other states, or aliens, in which latter case it shall have original but not exclusive jurisdiction. And shall

<small>Proceedings against public ministers.</small> have exclusively all such jurisdiction of suits or proceedings against ambassadors, or other public ministers, or their domestics, or domestic servants as a court of law can have or exercise consistently with the law of nations; and original, but not exclusive jurisdiction of all suits brought by ambassadors, or other public ministers, or in which a consul, or vice-consul, shall be a party. And the trial of issues in fact in the supreme court, in all actions

at law against citizens of the United States, shall be by jury. The supreme court shall also have appellate jurisdiction from the circuit courts and courts of the several states, in the cases herein after specially provided for: And shall have power to issue writs of prohibition to the district courts, when proceeding as courts of admiralty and maritime jurisdiction, and writs of *mandamus*, in cases warranted by the principles and usages of law, to any courts appointed, or persons holding office, under the authority of the United States.

Supreme court appellate jurisdiction.

Sec. 14. *And be it further enacted*, That all the beforementioned courts of the United States, shall have power to issue writs of *scire facias*, *habeas corpus*, and all other writs not specially provided for by statute, which may be necessary for the exercise of their respective jurisdictions, and agreeable to the principles and usages of law. And that either of the justices of the supreme court, as well as judges of the district courts, shall have power to grant writs of *habeas corpus* for the purpose of an enquiry into the cause of commitment.—*Provided*, That writs of *habeas corpus*, shall in no case extend to prisoners in gaol, unless where they are in custody, under or by colour of the authority of the United States, or are committed for trial before some court of the same, or are necessary to be brought into court to testify.

Courts of U. States issue writs scire facias, &c.

Justices and judges same power.

Sec. 15. *And be it further enacted*, That all the said courts of the United States, shall have power in the trial of actions at law, on motion and due notice thereof being given, to require the parties to produce books or writings in their possession or power, which contain evidence pertinent to the issue, in cases and under circumstances where they might be compelled to produce the same by the ordinary rules of proceeding in chancery; and if a plaintiff shall fail to comply with such order, to

Parties shall produce books and writings.

produce books or writings, it shall be lawful for th
courts respectively, on motion, to give the lik
judgment for the defendant as in cafes of nonfuit
and if a defendant shall fail to comply with such or
der, to produce books or writings, it shall be law
ful for the courts respectively on motion as afore
said, to give judgment against him or her by de
fault.

<small>Suits in equity limited.</small> Sec. 16. *And be it further enacted,* That fuits i equity shall not be fuftained in either of the court of the United States, in any cafe where plain, ade quate, and complete remedy may be had at law.

<small>Courts of U. States may grant new trials.</small> Sec. 17. *And be it further enacted,* That all th said courts of the United States shall have powe to grant new trials, in cafes where there has bee a trial by jury for reafons for which new trial have ufually been granted in the courts of law and shall have power to impofe and adminifter al neceffary oaths or affirmations, and to punifh b fine or imprifonment, at the difcretion of said courts all contempts of authority in any caufe or hearin, before the fame; and to make and eftablifh all ne ceffary rules for the orderly conducting bufinefs i the said courts, provided fuch rules are not repug nant to the laws of the United States.

<small>Execution may be ftayed in cafe.</small> Sec. 18. *And be it further enacted,* That whei in a circuit court, judgment upon a verdict in civil action shall be entered, execution may on mo tion of either party, at the difcretion of the court and on fuch conditions for the fecurity of the ad verfe party as they may judge proper, be ftayed for ty-two days from the time of entering judgment to give time to file in the clerk's office of said court a petition for a new trial. And if fuch petition be there filed within said term of forty-two days, with a certificate thereon from either of the judges o fuch court, that he allows the fame to be filed which certificate he may make or refufe at his dif

retion, execution shall of course be further stayed to the next session of said court. And if a new trial be granted, the former judgment shall be thereby rendered void.

Sec. 19. *And be it further enacted,* That it shall be the duty of circuit courts, in causes in equity and of admiralty and maritime jurisdiction, to cause the facts on which they found their sentence or decree, fully to appear upon the record either from the pleadings and decree itself, or a state of the case agreed by the parties, or their council, or if they disagree by a stating of the case by the court. Facts to appear on record.

Sec. 20. *And be it further enacted,* That where in a circuit court, a plaintiff in an action, originally brought there, or a petitioner in equity, other than the United States, recovers less than the sum or value of five hundred dollars, or a libellant, upon his own appeal, less than the sum or value of three hundred dollars, he shall not be allowed, but at the discretion of the court, may be adjudged to pay costs. Costs not allowed unless recover 500 dollars.

Sec. 21. *And be it further enacted,* That from final decrees in a district court in causes of admiralty and maritime jurisdiction, where the matter in dispute exceeds the sum or value of three hundred dollars, exclusive of costs, an appeal shall be allowed to the next circuit court, to be held in such district. *Provided nevertheless,* That all such appeals from final decrees as aforesaid, from the district court of Main, shall be made to the circuit court, next to be holden after each appeal in the district of Massachusetts. Appeals where matter in dispute exceeds 300 dollars.

Sec. 22. *And be it further enacted,* That final decrees and judgments in civil actions in a district court, where the matter in dispute exceeds the sum or value of fifty dollars, exclusive of costs, may be re-examined, and reversed or affirmed in a circuit court, holden in the same district, upon a writ of Final decrees re-examined above 500 dollars.

error, whereto shall be annexed and returne[d] therewith at the day and place therein mentione[d] an authenticated transcript of the record, and assig[n]ment of errors, and prayer for reversal, with a cit[a]tion to the adverse party, signed by the judge [of] such district court, or a justice of the supreme cour[t,] the adverse party having at least twenty days notic[e.]

and suits in equity exceed the value of 2000 dollars. And upon a like process, may final judgments an[d] decrees in civil actions, and suits in equity in a ci[r]cuit court, brought there by original process, [or] removed there from courts of the several states, [or] removed there by appeal from a district court whe[re] the matter in dispute exceeds the sum or value [of] two thousand dollars, exclusive of costs, be re-e[x]amined and reversed or affirmed in the supren[e] court, the citation being in such case signed by [a] judge of such circuit court, or justice of the supren[e] court, and the adverse party having at least thir[ty] days notice. But there shall be no reversal in e[i]ther court on such writ of error for error in ruli[ng] any plea in abatement, other than a plea to the j[u]risdiction of the court, or such plea to a petiti[on] or bill in equity, as in the nature of a demurrer, [or]

Writs of error limited. for any error in fact. And writs of error shall n[ot] be brought but within five years after renderi[ng] or passing the judgment or decree complained [of,] or in case the person entitled to such writ of err[or] be an infant, *feme covert non compos mentis*, or i[m]prisoned, then within five years as aforesaid, excl[u]sive of the time of such disability. And every ju[s]

Plaintiff to give security. tice or judge signing a citation on any writ of err[or] as aforesaid, shall take good and sufficient securit[y] that the plaintiff in error shall prosecute his writ [to] effect, and answer all damages and costs if he f[ail] to make his plea good.

Writs of error of a supersedeas in lease. Sec. 23. *And be it further enacted*, That a w[rit] of error as aforesaid shall be a supersedeas and st[ay] execution in cases only where the writ of error [is] served, by a copy thereof being lodged for the a[dverse]

[135]

erse party in the clerk's office where the record remains, within ten days, Sundays exclusive, after rendering the judgment or passing the decree complained of. Until the expiration of which term of ten days, executions shall not issue in any case where a writ of error may be a supersedeas; and whereupon such writ of error the supreme or a circuit court shall affirm a judgment or decree, they shall adjudge or decree to the respondent in error just damages for his delay, and single or double costs at their discretion.

Sec. 24. *And be it further enacted,* That when judgment or a decree shall be reversed in a circuit court, such court shall proceed to render such judgment or pass such decree as the district court should have rendered or passed; and the supreme court shall do the same on reversals therein, except where the reversal is in favor of the plaintiff, or petitioner in the original suit, and the damages to be assessed, or matter to be decreed, are uncertain, in which case they shall remand the cause for a final decision. And the supreme court shall not issue execution in causes that are removed before them by writs of error, but shall send a special mandate to the circuit court to award execution thereupon. *Judgment or decree reversed. Supreme Court not issue execution.*

Sec. 25. *And be it further enacted,* That a final judgment or decree in any suit, in the highest court of law or equity of a state in which a decision in the suit could be had, where is drawn in question the validity of a treaty or statute of, or an authority exercised under the United States, and the decision is against their validity; or where is drawn in question the validity of a statute of, or an authority exercised under any state, on the ground of their being repugnant to the constitution, treaties or laws of the United States, and the decision is in favor of such their validity, or where is drawn in question the construction of any clause of the Constitution, or of a treaty, or statute of, or commis- *Where validity of a treaty is questioned, cause may be re-examined.*

sion held under the United States, and the decisio[r]
is against the title, right, privilege or exemptio[n]
specially set up or claimed by either party, unde[r]
such clause of the said Constitution, treaty, statut[e]
or commission, may be re-examined and reverse[d]
or affirmed in the supreme court of the Unite[d]
States upon a writ of error, the citation being sign[-]
ed by the chief justice, or judge or chancellor [of]
the court rendering or passing the judgment or de[-]
cree complained of, or by a justice of the suprem[e]
court of the United States, in the same manner an[d]
under the same regulations, and the writ shall hav[e]
the same effect, as if the judgment or decree com[-]
plained of had been rendered or passed in a circu[it]
court, and the proceeding upon the reversal sha[ll]

Proceedings on reversal.

also be the same, except that the supreme cour[t]
instead of remanding the cause for a final decision [as]
before provided, may at their discretion, if th[e]
cause shall have been once remanded before, pr[o-]
ceed to a final decision of the same, and awa[rd]

No writs of error but as above mentioned.

execution. But no other error shall be assigned [or]
regarded as a ground of reversal in any such ca[use]
as aforesaid, than such as appears on the face [of]
the record, and immediately respects the befor[e]
mentioned questions of validity or construction [of]
the said Constitution, treaties, statutes, commission[s]
or authorities in dispute.

In cases of forfeiture the courts may give judgment in equity.

Sec. 26. *And be it further enacted*, That in a[ll]
cases brought before either of the courts of th[e]
United States to recover the forfeiture annexed [to]
any articles of agreement, covenant, bond, or oth[er]
speciality, where the forfeiture, breach or non-pe[r-]
formance shall appear, by the default or confessio[n]
of the defendant, or upon demurrer, the court b[e-]
fore whom the action is, shall render judgme[nt]
therein for the plaintiff to recover so much as is d[ue]
according to equity. And when the sum f[or]

Sum assessed by jury.

which judgment should be rendered is uncertai[n]

the fame fhall, if either of the parties requeſt it be aſſeſſed by a jury.

Sec. 27. *And be it further enacted,* That a mar- <small>Marſhal ap-</small>
fhal fhall be appointed in and for each diſtrict for <small>pointed.</small>
the term of four years, but fhall be removeable from
office at pleaſure, whoſe duty it fhall be to attend
the diſtrict and circuit courts when fitting therein,
and alſo the ſupreme court in the diſtrict in which
that court fhall fit. And to execute throughout
the diſtrict, all lawful precepts directed to him, and
iſſued under the authority of the United States, and
he fhall have power to command all neceſſary aſ-
ſiſtance in the execution of his duty, and to appoint as there fhall be occaſion, one or more deputies, who fhall be removeable from office by the
judge of the diſtrict court, or the circuit court fitting within the diſtrict, at the pleaſure of either,
and before he enters on the duties of his office, he
fhall become bound for the faithful performance of
the fame, by himſelf and by his deputies before the
judge of the diſtrict court to the United States,
jointly and ſeverally, with two good and fufficient
ſureties, inhabitants and freeholders of fuch diſtrict,
to be approved by the diſtrict judge in the ſum of
twenty thouſand dollars, and fhall take before faid
judge, as fhall alſo his deputies, before they enter <small>Marſhal.</small>
on the duties of their appointment, the following
oath of office: "I, A. B. do ſolemnly ſwear or <small>His oath.</small>
affirm, that I will faithfully execute all lawful precepts directed to the marſhall of the diſtrict of
            under the authority of the United States,
and true returns make, and in all things well and
truly, and without malice or partiality, perform the
duties of the office of marſhall (or marſhall's deputy, as the caſe may be) of the diſtrict of
during my continuance in faid office, and take only
my lawful fees. So help me God."

Sec. 28. *And be it further enacted,* That in all <small>Marſhall a</small>
cauſes wherein the marſhall or his deputy fhall be a <small>party.</small>

party, the writs and precepts therein shall be directed to such disinterested person as the court, or any justice or judge thereof may appoint, and the person so appointed, is hereby authorised to execute and return the same. And in case of the death of any marshall, his deputy or deputies shall continue in office, unless otherwise specially removed; and shall execute the same in the name of the deceased, until another marshall be appointed and sworn:

Defaults of deputies. And the defaults or misfeasances in office of such deputy or deputies in the mean time, as well as before, shall be adjudged a breach of the condition of the bond given, as before directed, by the marshall who appointed them; and the executor or

Executor or adminiſtrator of deceased marſhalls. administrator of the deceased marshall shall have like remedy for the defaults and misfeasances in office of such deputy or deputies during such interval, as they would be entitled to if the marshall had continued in life and in the exercise of his said office, until his successor was appointed, and sworn or affirmed: And every marshall or his deputy when removed from office, or when the term for which the marshall is appointed shall expire, shall have power notwithstanding to execute all such precepts as may be in their hands respectively at the time of such removal or expiration of office; and the marshall shall be held answerable for the deli-

Marſhalls power after removal. very to his successor of all prisoners which may be in his custody at the time of his removal, or when the term for which he is appointed shall expire, and for that purpose may retain such prisoners in his custody until his successor shall be appointed and qualified as the law directs.

Caſes puniſhable with death be had in county. Sec. 29. *And be it further enacted,* That in cases punishable with death, the trial shall be had in the county where the offence was committed, or where that cannot be done without great inconvenience, twelve petit jurors at least shall be summoned from thence. And jurors in all cases to serve in the

nited States shall be designated by
in each state respectively according
forming juries therein now practi-
e laws of the same shall render such
cticable by the courts or marshalls
tates ; and the jurors shall have the
ons as are requisite for jurors by the   Jurors by lot.
 of which they are citizens, to serve
ourts of law of such state, and shall
ere shall be occasion for them, from
e district om time to time as the
ct, so as shall be most favorable to
al, and so as not to incur an unne-
, or unduly to burthen the citizens
he district with such services. And
facias when directed by the court   Writs ve-
the clerk's office, and shall be served   nire facias from clerk's
y the marshall in his proper person,   office.
y, or in case the marshall or his de-
 indifferent person, or is interested
 the cause, by such fit person as the
cially appoint for that purpose, to
ll administer an oath or affirmation
ly and impartially serve and return
d when from challenges or other-
not be a jury to determine any civil
se, the marshall or his deputy shall,
e court where such defect of jurors
turn jurymen *de talibus circumstan-*   Juries de talibus, &c.
o complete the pannel ; and when
his deputy are disqualified as afore-
y be returned by such disinterested
ourt shall appoint.

{nd be it further enacted, That the   Mode of proof.
by oral testimony and examination
open court shall be the same in all
e United States, as well in the trial
uity and of admiralty and maritime
 of actions at common law. And

when the testimony of any person shall be necessary in any civil cause depending in any district in any court of the United States, who shall live at a greater distance from the place of trial than one hundred miles, or is bound on a voyage to sea, or is about to go out of the United States, or out of such district, and to a greater distance from the place of trial than as aforesaid, before the time of trial, or is ancient or very infirm, the deposition of such person may be taken *de bene esse* before any justice or judge of any of the courts of the United States, or before any chancellor, justice or judge of a supreme or superior court, mayor or chief magistrate of a city, or judge of a county court or court of common pleas of any of the United States, not being of counsel or attorney to either of the parties, or interested in the event of the cause, provided that a notification from the magistrate before whom the deposition is to be taken to the adverse party, to be present at the taking of the same, and to put interrogatories, if he think fit, be first made out and served on the adverse party or his attorney as either may be nearest, if either is within one hundred miles of the place of such caption, allowing time for their attendance after notified, not less than at the rate of one day, Sundays exclusive, for every twenty miles travel. And in causes of admiralty and maritime jurisdiction, or other cases of seizure when a libel shall be filed, in which an adverse party is not named, and depositions of persons circumstanced as aforesaid shall be taken before a claim be put in, the like notification as aforesaid shall be given to the person having the agency or possession of the property libelled at the time of the capture or seizure of the same, if known to the libellant. And every person deposing as aforesaid shall be carefully examined and cautioned, and sworn or affirmed to testify the whole truth, and shall subscribe the testimony by him or her given after the

Deposition de bene esse.

Adverse party notified.

Admiralty and maritime causes.

Agent notified.

ame shall be reduced to writing, which shall be done only by the magistrate taking the deposition, or by the deponent in his presence. And the de- *Depositions retained.* positions so taken shall be retained by such magistrate until he deliver the same with his own hand into the court for which they are taken, or shall, together with a certificate of the reasons as aforesaid of their being taken, and of the notice if any given to the adverse party, be by him the said magistrate sealed up and directed to such court, and remain under his seal until opened in court. And any person may be compelled to appear and depose as aforesaid in the same manner as to appear and testify in court. And in the trial of any cause of admi- *Appeal allowed.* ralty or maritime jurisdiction in a district court, the decree in which may be appealed from, if either party shall suggest to and satisfy the court that probably it will not be in his power to produce the witnesses there testifying before the circuit court should an appeal be had, and shall move that their testimony be taken down in writing, it shall be so done by the clerk of the court. And if an appeal be had, such testimony may be used on the trial of the same, if it shall appear to the satisfaction of the court which shall try the appeal, that the witnesses are then dead or gone out of the United States, or to a greater distance than as aforesaid from the place where the court is sitting, or that by reason of age, sickness, bodily infirmity or imprisonment, they are unable to travel and appear at court, *Depositions used in case of sickness, death, &c.* but not otherwise. And unless the same shall be made to appear on the trial of any cause, with respect to witnesses whose depositions may have been taken therein, such depositions shall not be admitted or used in the cause. *Provided*, That nothing herein shall be construed to prevent any court of *Dedimus potestatem as usual.* the United States from granting a *dedimus potestatem* to take depositions according to common usage, when it may be necessary to prevent a failure or de-

lay of juftice; which power they fhall feverally poſ-
feſs, nor to extend to depofitions taken in *perpetuaˆ
rei memoriam,* which if they relate to matters thaˆ
may be cognizable in any court of the United Stateſ
a circuit court on application thereto made as a couˆ
of equity, may, according to the ufages in chancerˆ
direct to be taken.

Sec. 31. *And be it enacted,* That where any fuː
fhall be depending in any court of the United Stateˆ
and either of the parties fhall die before final judgˆ

Executor or adminiftrator may profecute and defend. ment, the executor or adminiftrator of fuch deceaˆ ed party who was plaintiff, petitioner, or defencˆ ant, in cafe the caufe of action doth by law furˆ vive, fhall have full power to profecute or defenˆ any fuch fuit or action until final judgment; anˆ the defendant or defendants are hereby obliged tˆ anfwer thereto accordingly; and the court beforˆ whom fuch caufe may be depending, is hereby emˆ powered and directed to hear and determine thˆ fame, and to render judgment for or againft thˆ executor or adminiftrator, as the cafe may requirˆ And if fuch executor or adminiftrator having beeˆ duly ferved with a *fcire facias* from the office of thˆ clerk of the court where fuch fuit is dependingˆ twenty days beforehand, fhall neglect or refufe tˆ become a party to the fuit, the court may rendeˆ judgment againft the eftate of the deceafed partyˆ in the fame manner as if the executor or adminiˆ trator had voluntarily made himfelf a party to thˆ

Executor and adminiftrator may have continuance. fuit: And the executor or adminiftrator who fhaˆ become a party as aforefaid, fhall, upon motion tˆ the court where the fuit is depending, be entitleˆ to a continuance of the fame until the next term oˆ

Two plaintiffs. the faid court. And if there be two or more plainˆ tiffs or defendants, and one or more of them fhaˆ die, if the caufe of action fhall furvive to the furˆ viving plaintiff or plaintiffs, or againft the furvivˆ ing defendant or defendants, the writ or action fhaˆ not be thereby abated; but fuch death being fugˆ

gested upon the record, the action shall proceed at the suit of the surviving plaintiff or plaintiffs against the surviving defendant or defendants. *Surviving plaintiff may continue suit.*

Sec. 32. *And be it further enacted,* That no summons, writ, declaration, return, process, judgment, or other proceedings in civil causes in any of the courts of the United States, shall be abated, arrested, quashed or reversed, for any defect or want of form, but the said courts respectively shall proceed and give judgment according as the right of the cause and matter in law shall appear unto them, without regarding any imperfections, defects, or want of form in such writ, declaration or other pleading, return, process, judgment, or course of proceeding whatsoever, except those only in cases of demurrer, which the party demurring shall specially sit down and express together with his demurrer as the cause thereof. And the said courts respectively shall and may, by virtue of this act, from time to time, amend all and every such imperfections, defects and want of form, other than those only which the party demurring shall express as aforesaid, and may at any time permit either of the parties to amend any defect in the process or pleadings, upon such conditions as the said courts respectively shall in their discretion, and by their rules prescribe. *Writs shall not abate for defect of form. Courts may amend imperfections.*

Sec. 33. *And be it further enacted,* That for any crime or offence against the United States, the offender may, by any justice or judge of the United States, or by any justice of the peace, or other magistrate of any of the United States where he may be found agreeably to the usual mode of process against offenders in such state, and at the expence of the United States, be arrested, and imprisoned or bailed, as the case may be, for trial before such court of the United States as by this act has cognizance of the offence : And copies of the process shall be returned as speedily as may be into the clerk's office *Criminals against the United States arrested by any justice of the peace. Recognizance returned to the clerk's office.*

of such court, together with the recognizances of the witnesses for their appearance to testify in the case; which recognizances the magistrate before whom the examination shall be, may require on pain of imprisonment. And if such commitment of the offender, or the witnesses shall be in a district other than that in which the offence is to be tried, it shall be the duty of the judge of that district where the delinquent is imprisoned, seasonably to issue, and of the marshall of the same district to execute, a warrant for the removal of the offender, and the witnesses, or either of them, as the case may be, to the district in which the trial is to be had. And upon all arrests in criminal cases, bail shall be admitted, except where the punishment may be death, in which cases it shall not be admitted but by the supreme or a circuit court, or by a justice of the supreme court, or a judge of a district court, who shall exercise their discretion therein, regarding the nature and circumstances of the offence, and of the evidence, and the usages of law. And if a person committed by a justice of the supreme or a judge of a district court for an offence not punishable with death, shall afterwards procure bail, and there be no judge of the United States in the district to take the same, it may be taken by any judge of the supreme, or superior court of law of such state.

Offender may be removed by warrant.

Bail admitted.

Bail, how taken in case.

Laws of states, rules of decision.

Sec. 34. *And be it further enacted,* That the laws of the several states, except where the constitution treaties or statutes of the United States shall otherwise require or provide, shall be regarded as rules of decision in trials at common law in the courts of the United States in cases where they apply.

Parties manage their own cause.

Sec. 35. *And be it further enacted,* That in all the courts of the United States, the parties may plead and manage their own causes personally or by the assistance of such counsel or attornies at law as by the rules of the said courts respectively shall be permitted to manage and conduct causes there-

n. And there shall be appointed in each district a meet person learned in the law to act as attorney for the United States in such district, who shall be sworn or affirmed to the faithful execution of his office, whose duty it shall be to prosecute in such district all delinquents for crimes and offences, cognizable under the authority of the United States, and all civil actions in which the United States, shall be concerned, except before the supreme court in the district in which that court shall be holden. And he shall receive as a compensation for his services such fees as shall be taxed therefor in the respective courts before which the suits or prosecutions shall be. And there shall also be appointed a meet person, learned in the law, to act as attorney-general for the United States, who shall be sworn or affirmed, to a faithful execution of his office; whose duty it shall be to prosecute and conduct all suits in the supreme court in which the United States shall be concerned, and to give his advice and opinion upon questions of law when required by the President of the United States, or when requested by the heads of any of the departments, touching any matters that may concern their departments, and shall receive such compensation for his services as shall by law be provided. *Attorney for each district.*

Attorney-general.

FREDERICK AUGUSTUS MUHLENBERG,

Speaker of the House of Representatives.

JOHN ADAMS, *Vice-President of the United States,*

and President of the Senate.

Approved, September the 24th, 1789.

GEORGE WASHINGTON,

President of the United States.

CHAPTER XXI.

An ACT *to regulate* PROCESSES *in the* COURTS *the United States.*

<small>Test of writs.</small>

Section 1. BE *it enacted by the* SENATE *and* House *of* REPRESENTATIVES *of the United States of America in Congress assembled,* That all writ and processes issuing from a supreme or a circuit court, shall bear test of the chief justice of the supreme court, and if from a district court, shall bear test of the judge of such court, and shall be under the seal of the court from whence they issue; and signed by the clerk thereof. The seals of the supreme and circuit courts, to be provided by the supreme court and of the district courts, by the respective judges of the same.

<small>Seals.</small>

<small>Forms of writs as in the respective states.</small>

<small>Admiralty according to the forms civil law.</small>

<small>Fees.</small>

Sec. 2. *And be it further enacted,* That until further provision shall be made, and except where by this act or other statutes of the United States is otherwise provided, the forms of writs and executions, except their style, and modes of process and rates of fees, except fees to judges, in the circuit and district courts, in suits at common law, shall be the same in each state respectively as are now used or allowed in the supreme courts of the same. And the forms and modes of proceedings in causes of equity, and of admiralty and maritime jurisdiction shall be according to the course of the civil law. And the rates of fees the same as are or were last allowed by the states respectively in the court exercising supreme jurisdiction in such causes. *Provided,* That on judgments in any of the cases aforesaid where different kinds of executions are issuable in succession, a *capias ad satisfaciendum* being one the plaintiff shall have his election to take out *capias ad satisfaciendum* in the first instance, and be at liberty to pursue the same until a tender of the debt and costs in gold or silver shall be made,

Sec. 3. *And be it further enacted,* That this act shall continue in force until the end of the next session of Congress, and no longer. **Limitation.**

FREDERICK AUGUSTUS MUHLENBERG,
Speaker of the House of Representatives.

JOHN ADAMS, *Vice-President of the United States,
and President of the Senate.*

APPROVED, September the 29th, 1789.

GEORGE WASHINGTON,
President of the United States.

CHAPTER XXII.

An ACT *to explain and amend an Act, entitled,* " An Act for Registering and Clearing VESSELS, Regulating the COASTING TRADE, and for other Purposes."

Section 1. BE *it enacted by the* SENATE *and* HOUSE *of* REPRESENTATIVES *of the United States of America in Congress assembled,* That when any goods, wares or merchandize of foreign growth or manufacture, shall be unladen from any ship or vessel in virtue of a permit obtained for that purpose, and shall be put into a craft or vessel, with intent to be transported to a landing within the same district, it shall be the duty of the inspector, or other officer attending the unlading of such goods, wares and merchandize, to deliver to the master or commander of every such craft or vessel, a certificate of such goods, wares and merchandize, having been duly entered, and a permit granted therefor; and such certificate shall contain a description of all the packages with their marks and numbers, and shall authorize the transportation and landing of the same, at any landing within the same district, without any further fee or permit, any thing in the said recited act to the contrary notwithstanding. **Goods unladen by permit and transported to a landing in the same district, to be accompanied with a certificate from the inspector or other proper officer.**

[148]

Exemption of veſſels under 20 tons, from entering and clearing extended to veſſels of 50 tons having on board goods, &c. of the growth or produce of the United States.

Sec. 2. *And be it further enacted,* That ſo muc[h] of the twenty-ſecond ſection of the ſaid recited ac[t] as exempts veſſels of leſs than twenty, and not le[ſs] than five tons burthen, employed between any [of] the diſtricts of the United States, in any bay or r[i]ver, and having a licence from the collector of th[e] diſtrict to which ſuch veſſel belongs, from enterin[g] and clearing for the term of one year, be extende[d] to veſſels not exceeding fifty tons: *Provided,* ſuc[h] veſſels ſhall not have on board goods, wares [or] merchandize, other than ſuch as are actually th[e] growth or produce of the United States.

Ruble of Ruſſia, rate of, repealed.

Sec. 3. *And be it further enacted,* That ſo muc[h] of an act, entitled, " An act to regulate the colle[c]tion of the duties impoſed by law on the tonna[ge] of ſhips or veſſels, and on goods, wares and me[r]chandizes imported into the United States," hath rated the ruble of Ruſſia at one hundred cen[ts] be, and the ſame is hereby repealed and made n[ull] and void.

FREDERICK AUGUSTUS MUHLENBER[G]
Speaker of the Houſe of Repreſentatives.

JOHN ADAMS, *Vice-Preſident of the United Stat[es]*
and Preſident of the Senate.

APPROVED, September the 29th, 1789.

GEORGE WASHINGTO[N]
Preſident of the United States.

CHAPTER XXIII.

An ACT *making* APPROPRIATIONS *for the Serv.[ice] of the preſent Year.*

Specific appropriations of money for expences of civil liſt and war department;

Section 1. BE it enacted by the SENATE and Hou[ſe] of REPRESENTATIVES of the Unit[ed] States of America in Congreſs aſſembled, That the[re] be appropriated for the ſervice of the preſent yea[r,] to be paid out of the monies which ariſe, either fro[m] the requiſitions heretofore made upon the ſever[al] tates, or from the duties on impoſt and tonnage, the following ſums, viz. A ſum not exceeding two hundred and ſixteen thouſand dollars for defraying the expences of the civil liſt, under the late and preſent government; a ſum not exceeding one hundred and thirty-ſeven thouſand dollars for defraying the expences of the department of war; a ſum not exceeding one hundred and ninety thouſand dollars for diſcharging the warrants iſſued by the late board of treaſury, and remaining unſatisfied; and a ſum not exceeding ninety-ſix thouſand dollars for paying the penſions to invalids. *alſo to diſcharge warrants of late board of treaſury, & for penſions to invalids.*

FREDERICK AUGUSTUS MUHLENBERG,
Speaker of the Houſe of Repreſentatives.

JOHN ADAMS, *Vice-Preſident of the United States,
and Preſident of the Senate.*

APPROVED, September the 29th, 1789.

GEORGE WASHINGTON,
Preſident of the United States.

CHAPTER XXIV.

An ACT *providing for the* PAYMENT *of the* INVALID PENSIONERS *of the United States.*

Section 1. **B**E *it enacted by the* SENATE *and* HOUSE *of* REPRESENTATIVES *of the United States of America in Congreſs aſſembled,* That the Military Penſions which have been granted and paid by the States reſpectively, in purſuance of the acts of the United States in Congreſs aſſembled, to the invalids who were wounded and diſabled during the late war, ſhall be continued and paid by the United States, from the fourth day of March laſt, for the *Military penſions heretofore paid by the ſtates to be paid from 4th March laſt for one year, and under what regulations.*

space of one year, under such regulations as the President of the United States may direct.

FREDERICK AUGUSTUS MUHLENBERG,
Speaker of the House of Representatives.

JOHN ADAMS, *Vice-President of the United States and President of the Senate.*

APPROVED, September the 29th, 1789.

GEORGE WASHINGTON
President of the United States.

CHAPTER XXV.

An ACT *to recognize and adapt to the Constitution of the United States the establishment of the* TROOPS *raised under the Resolves of the United States in Congress assembled, and for other Purposes therein mentioned.*

Section 1.

Establishment of 3d Oct. 1787, recognized for troops in the service of the United States.

BE *it enacted by the* SENATE *and* HOUSE *of* REPRESENTATIVES *of the United States of America in Congress assembled,* That the establishment contained in the resolve of the late Congress of the third day of October, one thousand seven hundred and eighty-seven, except as to the mode of appointing the officers, and also as is hereinafter provided, be, and the same is hereby recognized to be the establishment for the troops in the service of the United States.

Pay and allowance of troops.

Sec. 2. *And be it further enacted,* That the pay and allowances of the said troops be the same as have been established by the United States in Congress assembled, by their resolution of the twelfth of April, one thousand seven hundred and eighty-five.

Sec. 3. *And be it further enacted,* That all commissioned and non-commissioned officers and privates, who are or shall be in the service of the United States, shall take the following oaths or affirmations, to wit: "I, A. B. do solemnly swear or affirm (as the case may be) that I will support the Constitution of the United States." "I, A. B. do solemnly swear or affirm (as the case may be) to bear true allegiance to the United States of America, and to serve them honestly and faithfully against all their enemies or opposers whatsoever, and to observe and obey the orders of the President of the United States of America, and the orders of the officers appointed over me."

To take oath to support the constitution & bear allegiance to the United States.

Sec. 4. *And be it further enacted,* That the said troops shall be governed by the rules and articles of war which have been established by the United States in Congress assembled, or by such rules and articles of war, as may hereafter by law be established.

Troops to be governed by rules and articles of war.

Sec. 5. *And be it further enacted,* That for the purpose of protecting the inhabitants of the frontiers of the United States from the hostile incursions of the Indians, the President is hereby authorised to call into service from time to time, such part of the militia of the states respectively, as he may judge necessary for the purpose aforesaid; and that their pay and subsistence while in service, be the same as the pay and subsistence of the troops above mentioned.

For protecting frontiers, President may call forth militia.

Their pay and subsistence.

Sec. 6. *And be it further enacted,* That this act shall continue and be in force until the end of the next session of Congress, and no longer.

Continuance of this act.

FREDERICK AUGUSTUS MUHLENBERG,
Speaker of the House of Representatives.

JOHN ADAMS, *Vice-President of the United States, and President of the Senate.*

APPROVED, September the 29th, 1789.

GEORGE WASHINGTON,
President of the United States.

CHAPTER XXVI.

An ACT *to allow the* BARON DE GLAUBECK *the pay of a Captain in the Army of the United States.*

Section 1. BE *it enacted by the* SENATE *and* HOUSE *of* REPRESENTATIVES *of the United States of America in Congress assembled,* That the pay of a captain in the army of the United States be allowed to the Baron de Glaubeck, from the ninth day of March, one thousand seven hundred and eighty-one, to the twenty-fourth day of August one thousand seven hundred and eighty-two, to be paid in the same manner as other foreign officers in the service of the United States have been paid.

FREDERICK AUGUSTUS MUHLENBERG,
Speaker of the House of Representatives.

JOHN ADAMS, *Vice-President of the United States and President of the Senate.*

APPROVED, September the 29th, 1789.

GEORGE WASHINGTON,
President of the United States.

CHAPTER XXVII.

An ACT *to alter the Time for the next* MEETING *of* CONGRESS.

Section 1. BE *it enacted by the* SENATE *and* HOUSE *of* REPRESENTATIVES *of the United States of America in Congress assembled,* That after the adjournment of the present session, the next meeting of Congress shall be on the first Monday in January next.

FREDERICK AUGUSTUS MUHLENBERG,
Speaker of the House of Representatives.

JOHN ADAMS, *Vice-President of the United States, and President of the Senate.*

APPROVED, September the 29th, 1789.

GEORGE WASHINGTON,
President of the United States.

CONGRESS of the UNITED STATES:
Begun and held at the City of New-York, on Wednesday, the fourth of March, one thousand seven hundred and eighty-nine.

RESOLVED, That the Survey directed by Congress in their act of June the sixth, one thousand seven hundred and eighty-eight, be made and returned to the Secretary of the Treasury without delay; and that the President of the United States be requested to appoint a fit person to complete the same, who shall be allowed five dollars per day whilst actually employed in the said service, with the expences necessarily attending the execution thereof.

  FREDERICK AUGUSTUS MUHLENBERG,
   Speaker of the House of Representatives.
  JOHN ADAMS, *Vice-President of the United States,*
   and President of the Senate.

APPROVED, August the 26th, 1789.
  GEORGE WASHINGTON,
   President of the United States.

RESOLVED *by the* SENATE *and* HOUSE *of* REPRESENTATIVES *of the United States of America in Congress assembled,* That it be recommended to the Legislatures of the several States to pass laws, making it expressly the duty of the keepers of their gaols, to receive and safe keep therein all prisoners committed under the authority of the United States, until they shall be discharged by the due course of the laws thereof, under the like penalties as in the case of prisoners committed under the authority of such States respectively; the United States to pay for the use and keeping of such gaols, at the rate of fifty cents per month for each prisoner that shall, under their authority, be committed thereto, during the time such prisoners shall be therein confined;

and also to support such of said prisoners as shall be com
mitted for offences.

    FREDERICK AUGUSTUS MUHLENBER(
     Speaker of the House of Representatives.
   JOHN ADAMS, *Vice-President of the United Stat*
     and President of the Senate.
Approved, September the 23d, 1789.
    GEORGE WASHINGTON,
     President of the United States.

RESOLVED, That it shall be the duty of the Secreta
of State, to procure from time to time such of t
Statutes of the several States as may not be in his office.
    FREDERICK AUGUSTUS MUHLENBER
     Speaker of the House of Representatives.
   JOHN ADAMS, *Vice-President of the United Sta*
     and President of the Senate.
Approved, September the 23d, 1789.
    GEORGE WASHINGTON
     President of the United States.

RESOLVED *by the* Senate *and* House *of* Repres1
  tatives *of the United States of America in Cong.*
assembled, That John White, late a commissioner to se
the accounts between the United States and the states
Pennsylvania, Delaware and Maryland, and his clerks, Jo
Wright and Joshua Dawson, be considered as in office u1
the fourth day of February, one thousand seven hund.
and eighty-nine.
    FREDERICK AUGUSTUS MUHLENBER
     Speaker of the House of Representatives.
   JOHN ADAMS, *Vice-President of the United Sta*
     and President of the Senate
Approved, September the 29th, 1789.
    GEORGE WASHINGTON
     President of the United States.

Congress of the United States:

begun and held at the City of New-York, on Wednesday, the fourth of March, one thousand seven hundred and eighty-nine.

The Conventions of a number of the States having at the time of their adopting the Constitution expressed a desire, in order to prevent misconstruction or abuse of its powers, that further declaratory and restrictive clauses should be added: And as extending the ground of public confidence in the government will best insure the beneficent ends of its institution—

RESOLVED by the SENATE and HOUSE of REPRESENTATIVES of the United States of America in Congress assembled, two thirds of both Houses concurring, That the following articles be proposed to the legislatures of the several states, as amendments to the Constitution of the United States, all or any of which articles, when ratified by three fourths of the said legislatures, to be valid to all intents and purposes, as part of the said Constitution, viz.

ARTICLES in Addition to, and Amendment of, the CONSTITUTION OF THE UNITED STATES OF AMERICA, proposed by Congress, and ratified by the Legislatures of the several States, pursuant to the fifth article of the original Constitution.

Article the First.

After the first enumeration required by the first article of the Constitution, there shall be one Representative for every thirty thousand, until the number shall amount to one hundred, after which the proportion shall be so regulated by Congress, that there shall be not less than one hundred Representatives, nor less than one Representative for every forty thousand persons, until the number of Representatives shall amount to two hundred; after which the proportion

shall be so regulated by Congress, that there shall not b
less than two hundred Representatives, nor more than on
Representative for every fifty thousand persons.

Article the Second.

No law varying the compensation for the services of th
Senators and Representatives, shall take effect, until a
election of Representatives shall have intervened.

Article the Third.

Congress shall make no law respecting an establishmer
of religion, or prohibiting the free exercise thereof, c
abridging the freedom of speech, or of the press; or th
right of the people peaceably to assemble, and to petitio
the government for a redress of grievances.

Article the Fourth.

A well regulated militia being necessary to the securit
of a free state, the right of the people to keep and bear arn
shall not be infringed.

Article the Fifth.

No soldier shall in time of peace be quartered in ar
house without the consent of the owner; nor in time
war, but in a manner to be prescribed by law.

Article the Sixth.

The right of the people to be secure in their person
houses, papers, and effects, against unreasonable search
and seizures, shall not be violated; and no warrants sha
issue, but upon probable cause, supported by oath or affi
mation, and particularly describing the place to be searche
and the persons or things to be seized.

Article the Seventh.

No person shall be held to answer for a capital, or othe
wise infamous crime, unless on a presentment or indictme
of a Grand Jury, except in cases arising in the land or nav
forces, or in the militia when in actual service in time
war or public danger; nor shall any person be subject f

the fame offence to be twice put in jeopardy of life or limb; nor shall be compelled in any criminal cafe to be a witnefs againft himfelf, nor be deprived of life, liberty or property, without due procefs of law; nor shall private property be taken for public ufe without juft compenfation.

Article the Eighth.

In all criminal profecutions the accufed fhall enjoy the right to a fpeedy and public trial, by an impartial jury of the ftate and diftrict wherein the crime fhall have been committed, which diftrict fhall have been previoufly afcertained by law, and to be informed of the nature and caufe of the accufation; to be confronted with the witneffes againft him; to have compulfory procefs for obtaining witneffes in his favor, and to have the affiftance of counfel for his defence.

Article the Ninth.

In fuits at common law, where the value in controverfy fhall exceed twenty dollars, the right of trial by jury fhall be preferved; and no fact, tried by a jury, fhall be otherwife re-examined in any court of the United States, than according to the rules of the common law.

Article the Tenth.

Exceffive bail fhall not be required, nor exceffive fines impofed, nor cruel and unufual punifhments inflicted.

Article the Eleventh.

The enumeration in the Conftitution, of certain rights, fhall not be conftrued to deny or difparage others retained by the people.

Article the Twelfth.

The powers not delegated to the United States by the Conftitution, nor prohibited by it to the States, are referved to the States refpectively, or to the people.

FREDERICK AUGUSTUS MUHLENBERG,
Speaker of the Houfe of Reprefentatives.
JOHN ADAMS, *Vice-Prefident of the United States,
and Prefident of the Senate.*

{ JOHN BECKLEY, *Clerk of the Houfe of Reprefentatives.*
{ SAMUEL A. OTIS, *Secretary of the Senate.*

DEPARTMENT of STATE, to wit.

I HEREBY certify that an edition of the Acts of Congress, passed at the session of the Congress which began on the 4th of March, 1789, as also of the Constitution of the United States, and of the articles proposed in amendment thereto, under the title of 'Acts passed at the first session of the Congress of the United States of America,' printed in this present year 1791, at Philadelphia, by Francis Childs and John Swaine, in 157 pages octavo, have, from page 5 to page 157, inclusive, been carefully collated, by sworn Clerks, with the original rolls deposited in the office of the Secretary of State, and that the following is a correct list of the Verbal Variations of the said printed edition from the rolls, those of Orthography not being noted, to wit:

Printed edition.		Rolls.	Printed edition.		Rolls.
Page.	Line.		Page.	Line.	
4,	33,	court	113,	1,	
5,	12,	be a party		9,	entitled	intituled
5,	31,	annexed Falmouth	147,	12,		
		annexed the town of Falmouth	148,	14,		
3,	27,	all the waters — all waters	85,	16,	or	and
7,	33,	such a voyage — such voyage	90,	29,	of such	of every such
5,	38,	collectors — collector	102,	34,	register	registry
7,	32,	and — with	115,	14,	18	twenty-second
3,	20,	upon goods — upon all goods	121,	31,	called the South	called South
	32,	an — a	122,	17,	Monday of	Monday in
1,	18,	of duties — of the duties	130,	5,	adverse party shall	adverse shall
7,	13,	half per — half a per	134,	23,	as in	as is in
6,	22,	present year — present	135,	13,	or a decree	or decree
2,	15,		entitled	intituled	138,	9,	marshal be	marshal shall be
1,	26,		143,	21,	want	wants
3,	19,		153,	26,	by the due	by due
4,	8,					

GIVEN under my hand at Philadelphia, this 3d day of August, 1791.

THOMAS JEFFERSON, *Secretary of State.*

www.ingramcontent.com/pod-product-compliance
Lightning Source LLC
Chambersburg PA
CBHW030307170426
43202CB00009B/897